MW01229675

ᒑ

BLUE

BOB

an anthology incited by

Bob Dylan

edited by Adam Van Winkle

Cowboy Jamboree Press

good grit lit.

First Edition

ISBN: 9798366492065

www.cowboyjamboreemagazine.com

Cover Design: Adam Van Winkle

Interior Design: Adam Van Winkle

Cowboy Jamboree Press

good grit lit.

All the people we used to know
They're an illusion to me now

–Bob Dylan

HEREIN

THE LAST OF THE BEST

Matthew Ingate

Leonard Cohen sings to you from a spiritual world, Tom Waits sings to you from the underworld; John Prine sings to you from the heart – from your heart and from his – while Townes Van Zandt sings to you from the end of a long, dust road. You can hear Johnny Cash in Folsom Prison; you can hear Elvis in the Heartbreak Hotel. You can hear Sinatra in the wee small hours and you can hear Hank Williams coughing away in the Tower of Song. Bob Dylan sings to you from all these places, and beyond.

Like all of us, Bob Dylan is only human, but at times he seems even to shift outside the boundaries of that definition. He is a creator of an unfathomable body of work; of music, of art, of literature, of whiskey, of movies, books and radio. He is a scholar and he is a sculptor. He's a historian and teacher. In his own words he is a trapeze artist. He is a father, a grandfather and a great-grandfather. He is a brother, and he may be an uncle. He may be a husband. Above all else, though, he is a spirit; he is a ghost and he haunts us all in different ways.

Even when you're in the room with him, when you can catch a glimpse of him through the darkness and light, he is simultaneously there and yet a million miles away.

He strolls, floats, into view on the stage after his band have already begun playing. The music he makes is always playing, somewhere; in this world or the next one, most likely from a previous world and what we can hear is like the fading echo of a star; an explosion from millennia past that leaves such an impression that we can still trace it through the night sky today.

He doesn't get introduced, he doesn't announce his arrival, he just turns up and joins in at the piano and sings his song. In a lot of cities, it isn't uncommon for people to have no idea he's even in town playing that night. The so called Never Ending Tour is a night circus; it quietly rolls into view, blows the roof off the theatre and packs up ready to move onto the next joint and do it all over again.

When you go and see one Bob Dylan, you are going to see every Bob Dylan there has been, you see the fading ghost of the last Bob Dylan and the birth of a brand new one. You catch glimpses through the night of all the famous Dylans; the early folk and blues singer, the rock icon, the traveling shaman, the spiritualist, the Jokerman and the thief. If you're unlucky some nights you'll catch a glimpse of the fallen icon, and when you're lucky you catch a glimpse of the icon he became once more, following the stunning comeback album, Time Out of Mind, in

1997 (one of many such stunning comebacks from a lifetime and career full of such comebacks. Somehow, despite being so revered, respected and acclaimed, Dylan always seems to have his back to the wall).

In combative interviews with journalists in 1965 and 1966, a favourite line of deflection from the young Dylan was to pull apart a question that had been put to him by declaring that "we all have our own definitions of all those words", one time going on to explain that when we each hear the word house it conjures up a different image of a house in all of our minds. Similarly, we all have our own definition of what and who Bob Dylan is. A Scarface Pacino? Godfather Brando? We all have our own version of him, but one thing is for sure – he is, as he says, the enemy of the unlived, meaningless life.

But it makes no sense to try and pin him down in one way any more than it does for the rest of us, to pin one singular definition on him or confine him to just one categorisation. Some will spend their lives trying to figure out who he is and what his message is but trying to unpick and unpack them all can leave you tangled up in a web of blues. It's better to stand back and take them all in at once. Maybe, once the paint on his last masterpiece has dried, the last line on his last song is written and there is no more whiskey in the jar, we will find that his greatest

11

work of art of all was the mosaic of the Bob Dylan character itself.

Similarly, Bob Dylan the character, the performer and Bob Dylan the regular man are surely two separate entities. One way of finding that division is in accounts given of him by those who know him. His friends and contemporaries describe him in private moments as being shy; of being introverted and of being sensitive, and of course, anyone who has the words of Forever Young, Sign on the Window or I've Made Up My Mind To Give Myself to You flowing through their blood is writing with a sensitive mind, but the man who writes these songs and the man who presents them on the stage seem like two separate people, again. When Dylan performs, even if he performs a song sensitively, he also performs it defiantly. He performs it powerfully and any shyness seems stripped away once he has a microphone at his mouth and a piano beneath his hands. He commented that there "weren't enough masks on that tour" when talking about The Rolling Thunder Revue, but he has had a range of Bob Dylan masks on for most every performance in his long, enduring career.

When he's wearing one, he commands the room; he commands the stage and, unlike Achilles, he has no weak spots. He presses on and on no matter what happens, as if that is how things were meant to go all along; whether a fan makes it onto the stage and joins him at the mic like in Holland in 1993, whether he forgets the words or the notes to the song he's singing or whether the electricity cuts out in the room like it did night after night in Spain in early 2018, he just keeps pressing on. He is an unstoppable force on the stage.

Perhaps the only time the man who wrote those songs, not the other who performs them, really appeared on the stage was in the early 90s, when the Never Ending Tour was still young. He had lost command of his voice; he'd lost command of his back catalogue and his sense of his own identity seemed to be fragile. He vacillated between the sublime and the shambolic on shows around this time, singing in a voice that only a fan could love and hitting all the right notes in one song before not hitting any in the next. In videos from the era, he looks the most human he ever has on stage; he looks fragile and he looks vulnerable. He looks shy and sensitive, and the humanity comes from the contrast with every other corner of his career where he is so powerful that it is frightening, so in control of the uncontrollable that it's hard to fathom that one single human being has so much force and intensity within them.

Perhaps it is that frightening self-confidence, the assurance in what he is doing that sets him apart from similar songwriters. His otherworldliness can come from his confidence that no matter how his song is sung, it *will* be sung come what may.

Even Tom Waits with his gruff, gin-soaked voice at times drops the hobo-charade on stage and sings innocently, tenderly. Leonard Cohen, mystical though he was, came down from the mountain to meet his fans at their level. John Prine was humanity personified when he sang and you can feel it in every note, but Dylan's detachment and ability to let the spirit of the song move through him, wash over him and his audience at once gives the ultimate otherworldly quality that is so unique to him. His confidence in his art, his drive to express it and his calling are clear. There are the greats, there are the ancients and then there is Bob Dylan, drifting like a satellite.

As always, though, no one sums up these points better than Dylan himself. This time, he's wearing the mask of Jack Fate at the conclusion of Masked & Anonymous as he says:

"I was always a singer and maybe no more than that. Sometimes it's not enough to know the meaning of things, sometimes we have to know what things don't mean as well. Like what does it mean to not know what the person you love is capable of? Things fall apart, especially all the neat order of rules and laws. The way we look at the world is the way we really are. See it from a fair garden and everything looks cheerful. Climb to a higher plateau and you'll see plunder and murder. Truth and beauty are in the eye of the beholder. I stopped trying to figure everything out a long time ago."

I HOPE YOU READ THIS AND FORGIVE ME FOR ONCE IN A WHILE MAYBE THINKING I WAS THE CHOSEN ONE

Reagan M. Sova

When I was five, I had a good friend, Haskell, couple years older, whose father up and left. Weeks came and went, months. It became clear he wasn't coming back. So Haskell and I got to investigating his things. Mainly his Playboys but also records. We'd sneak down into the cellar some days, get an eyeful and listen to records for hours, even if the summer sun was shining.

Well, one day in the cellar, Haskell put on *Blonde on Blonde.* "Rainy Day Women #12 & 35," the first track of that album, cranked up. The song romped in my head; I envisioned a mad carnival procession with guitars, snare drums, harmonicas, tubas, monkeys, elephants, bottles of gin, torches of fire, wild dancing like a parade in the street. Hobos. Travelers. At five, I wasn't even 100% sure what getting stoned was, but I did know, based on how I felt when that man sang, that they definitely did do it to you when you were trying to be so good. I asked Haskell after a dazed minute: "Who the fuck is this guy?"

Besides looking at photos of naked ladies, listening to records, playing basketball, lighting off fireworks, and ramping dirt bikes, the other favorite thing Haskell and I used to do was slice up carrots and apples with our jackknives and walk into the woods behind his house, through a quarter mile of trails, to a pasture where a farmer kept some horses. These beasts appeared 12 feet tall to me when I was five. They'd reach their giant, long faces over the electric fence, eat right off a flat palm. I really loved those horses. There were four of them. Funny thing was, we never even asked the farmer if we could feed them. I think we thought they were *our* friends, so what business was it of the farmer's if we gave them a snack?

The following Halloween, in the afternoon, we visited the horses with a brown sack of cut up carrots and apples. One stout horse whose back had been sagging, big belly, who appeared ancient, collapsed into some tall grass. Felled by the wind of time. We dashed over to the farmer's log home, knocked his door, and told him what we saw. He horned his feet into some boots and came out cocking a 9mm pistol, grumbling, "I knew this day was coming." A short, stocky man in a black sweatshirt, overalls, we followed him through a gate, into the pasture where he crouched next to the ailing beast. Petted his head.

"Don't look boys."

The horse labored to breathe. He was eyeing me. I began to cry.

"Let me... sing to him while you do it."

The farmer glanced at Haskell, as if he was my father, or someone who could grant permission. Haskell nodded, like to say it was ok.

"Alright," the farmer said, "better for you boys to learn now, death's a chain smoker. He lights 'em up one right after the other."

With a wobbling voice, I sang "Sad Eyed Lady of the Lowlands," and on the fourth line, the one about burial, the farmer dispatched our friend.

Walking back through the trails, Haskell said, "Well... I know what'll cheer us up."

It was the Playboys. And hot mulled wine we snaked from his mother's cauldron. He also put on a new record I hadn't heard. It was that boisterous carnival leader I was just singing, but he sounded much more serious, like a different person even. The songs, though, served as the perfect soundtrack for our somber, contemplative mood. Side one spun into its concluding tune, "A Hard Rain's a-Gonna Fall." I imbibed every line, meditating on every word; there was something deep in that song. Mystical. Later I learned that the poet Allen Ginsberg said when he first heard it, he wept. In the dim cellar that day, when Dylan sang the line about seeing the young child next to the dead pony, Haskell's wild wide eyes landed upon me.

"I saw him too."

Those words, the music, set my heart sailing like a ghost ship, like the oracle had come to town and shouted my name.

HOW AM I SUPPOSED TO GET ANY RIDING DONE?

Clem Flowers

& now there's just a rattling, all right? not like a gentle cuddle of the outside of your baby bed no this is a steam train taking Blind Willie to Statesboro because he forgot to turn the lamps down low this is this stampede of a hurricane running out to a pasture of plenty this is the thing to shake loose all the masters of war out the blues that left them tangled up along 56th & Wabasha & they're trying to knock us out our shelter from the storm blowing in this idiot wind out along desolation row & I know it's all over now, because things have changed and there's only so many ways to say I want you so many ways to sing a thin man's ballad so many ways to dance out from this simple twist of fate and now we're back in the buckets of rain and the moon makes the tarantula's web shine like a chrome horse left to run free now that the diplomat has gone the way of Mr. Jones & I know it's a promise to never hurt an honest man but the groom is still waiting at the altar after a third round of the changing of the guards as their mama had to leave back for the factory swing shift & daddy went back to the alley & the man in me would do anything but have another conversation with the someone who has a hold of my heart but one of us must know sooner or

later that Isis would return so tonight I'll be staying
here with you the couch is fine I would never expect
you to give up your big brass bed but sleep refuses
to call and now I see the Gates of Eden forming over
your big pile of records of Lomax Field Recordings
& prints of paintings by Woody up over your
alabaster hull and a sweetheart like you deserves
better than to have me desecrate this ratty haven
with my strange visions of God, the Devil, Johanna,
and the like and all I really want to do is go back
down to Acapulco so maybe I should just go my way
and let you go yours and we will be all the better for
it but one more cup of coffee before I go just falls into
one too many mornings of watching you put
memories away in that hand-me-down leopard-
skin-pillbox-hat & now you're playing Queen Jane
at the latest million dollar bash & I of course am the
jokerman & you give me drinks & tell me you know
I'll paint my masterpiece this 4th time around & I
need to get going on it once we get back home & do
all I can until the morning hits & I gotta go serve
somebody stuck inside of Mobile the same who left
my back pages to feed the pigs out on Maggie's farm
& we both pretend we're gonna stay forever young
as we crawl out your window to run down to the
jugglers & the clowns who are waiting to get the
brown paint slapped on their passports same as we
are & we ride & we ride & we ride down this belt of
rolling thunder until the wheels are on fire &
sometimes the grains of sand bloom into someone
new & other times the moneyed hands just laugh &

21

drop the whole box on me & you want another song from me until you gasp at the wound above my eye & I laugh because I've always just had a puncher's chance & I tell you it's all right but you insist on bringing it all back home because I'm bleeding & all that's left now is to grab every last drop of good feeling I can because I know you're gonna make me lonesome when you go

LESS FRAGILE THAN THEY LOOK

Michael Chin

I was in love with a red-haired girl named Blue.

She loved me, too.

Life got busy. We worked. We ate. We screwed. If we had the time for something else, we didn't have the money, or if we had the money, it meant we were both working and didn't have the time.

If Blue had it her way, we'd have still spent whole Saturdays sneaking between screens at the multiplex off the tickets we bought to a single movie. We would experiment with every coffee shop and taqueria in the city. We would drive down to Greenbelt and catch the train into DC to go to shows, to go to the museum, to get some decent dim sum in China Town.

But who has the energy?

I found my chance, though. My high school buddy Cheeks was starting to hit the big time, strumming his same folk-rock shtick he had since the old days. He got a deal with a little studio and they helped him get on the road. *Real hand to mouth sort of thing,* he told us all in a Facebook message, *I get a per diem, but after gas and a Happy Meal I'm on my own.*

He was asking for places to stay. Blue didn't take well to disruptions in her routines, so I was grateful when one of Cheeks' college friends put him up in Baltimore. I still got to look like a good guy telling him if his plans fell through there was always room on my couch, and of course I'd come to his show.

The stars lined up for the show. It fell on a Thursday night when Blue and I were both off, and all of Cheeks' originals were just the kind of music that Blue liked—that Jack Johnson, Matt Nathanson, *I'm a sensitive dude but I've still got hair on my chest* shit. And he played enough covers of Tom Petty and Bruce Springsteen and Bob Dylan to keep it fun for me.

Dylan was the key. Three years earlier, when I first started seeing Blue, I played "Tangled Up In Blue" for her. She'd somehow never heard it before and she let me fuck her sideways on the couch that night. Since then, it was our song, or as close as we had to something like that.

I'd first heard "Tangled" when Cheeks picked at it in the courtyard at school, when all of us guys huddled near him to get a piece of the girls crowding the guitar. I asked if he still played it. *Every show, brother*, he wrote back.

There it was. Written in the stars. A night out. Live music, and I knew the singer. Our song on the docket. All that lost romance and reservations evaporating in six-string chords.

24

*

She looked perfect. Blue wore a ribbed navy tank top cut so her arms were bare—that same porcelain white color I ran my tongue up and down the first time we fucked six years before. Cut low enough so her chest threatened to spill out. I stayed close. Held her hand on the walk from the garage to the front door where they checked IDs and stamped our hands. Little black kitty paws with claws.

The place looked perfect, too. It'd been years since we last went, but it was packed enough to feel like a big deal, empty enough I wouldn't need to elbow too much to get us close to the stage. And spotlights on stage were blue. Just perfect.

I bought each of us a pint of Nattie Boh because they were on dollar special but when I tried to hand Blue hers, she told me she wouldn't drink that shit.

What do you mean shit? I asked her. *It's good enough at home, ain't it?*

We're out.

She ordered herself an amaretto sour and put it on my tab without asking. I didn't say anything. The thing about Blue that I'd figured out years before was if she was in a bad mood, the worst thing to do was engage. You take her mind off it. Don't let it faze you. It'll pass. I alternated sips from my two beers to keep them level.

25

We walked toward the stage and Blue stopped. Didn't show any interest in getting closer. I wanted Cheeks to be able to see me. Maybe give us a shout out or a point or something before "Tangled Up in Blue." But it wouldn't matter until the show started so I let it slide.

"You see those speakers up there?"

Blue sucked up her drink through that cocktail straw. Five minutes in and it was half gone. Really plowing through it, like she was trying to cost me or to get obliterated or both.

"They're called monitors. They let Cheeks hear what we're hearing. Otherwise, he can get all messed up only hearing the guitar or only hearing the drums behind him." I had played roadie for Cheeks a few times back in the day and gleaned some tidbits. Blue didn't get to see me like that. Back when my muscles weren't covered in pudge and back when I knew an inkling of things more technical than how to reset our wireless router.

Next to us, there was another guy mansplaining about how beer bottles were less fragile than they looked in movies. The guy and his girl were both younger than us, both had that dopey look like they were really in love, her back to his chest, her neck craned to look back at him while he tipped back his tallboy. He went on, "Think about it. If the bottles broke as easy as they did in the movies, how would they ever make it from the bottling plant to the liquor store? You're telling me no truck driver has to slam on the brakes, and no stock boy drops a case along the way?"

Blue got up on her tiptoes so I'd hear her when she spoke. "How long is this show going to be?"

How long is it going to be? It hadn't even started yet, and there she was asking about when she could leave. "I don't know," I said. "But trust me, once he gets started, the time's going to fly. You'll love it." I got to reminiscing about all the old shows I used to go to. About the time Cheeks tried to get the girls in the crowd to throw their panties up on stage at him. No one bit, so he kept on riffing on it, pointing out girls one by one and asking why they wouldn't do it. Our buddy Tommy was already three sheets to the wind and right there, on the middle of the dancefloor, unbuckled his belt and wrestled off his jeans pulled off his boxers leg by leg and flung them on stage, just missing Cheeks. Cheeks yucked it up. Said *there's a committed fan! Now let's keep this party rocking!* And there was this blond with brown roots standing by Tommy, all crinkle nosed and trying to stay away from him. No surer way to draw Tommy's attention. He took his dick in his hand and asked her if she wanted a sip. Made like he was going to chase her and she threw her vodka cran in his face.

I figured the story would crack up Blue. In the early days, it felt like all we did was swap bar stories. All

27

the stupid things we'd done coming back to us in this whirl of nostalgia. One story sets up the next, and even when she thought I was being an idiot, she'd still slug me in the shoulder and transition, *if you think that's bad...*

"That's disgusting," Blue said. No follow up. No transition.

"We were kids."

"It's sexual harassment. I hope he got thrown in jail," she said. "And what's the big idea telling me about you and your friends chasing girls? You think I want to hear about that?"

"Are you menstruating or something?"

She threw her drink in my face. A half-full, $10.50 tumbler, so it felt like five dollars of my own money dripping down my cheek. "I'm going to the bathroom."

I didn't try to stop her. I'm embarrassed to say it, but that kind of behavior turned me on more. Reminded me of when we'd fight in those early days, after the niceties were out of the way, but we were still young and fiery, still new to one another's bodies. We were usually at her place and she'd try to get me to leave and I'd kiss her and we'd wind up humping on the kitchen floor.

But then Cheeks came on stage. No opener, just the man himself with his drummer and a bass player.

People whistled and clapped their hands, and I figured Blue would turn back so she didn't miss anything.

"How y'all feeling tonight?"

More cheers. Cheeks ran a finger up and down the frets on his acoustic guitar. He'd always do that, on stage and in his living room, this barely audible whine of sound, lent extra volume now through the cord running from guitar to amplifier.

Everything about him was bigger—not just that sound, but his shoulders fuller, biceps bulging from a navy T-shirt, his hair bushier. He'd grown into himself. Looked every bit the traveling musician. And yet I knew him. Had been in the trenches hauling speakers and coils of wire and guitar cases. Had cheered him on loud when all he could get was twelve minutes at the rinky-dink open mic nights they used to run at the coffee shop on Varick Street, where the manager made us all order something to eat or he said we'd have to leave.

Here was Cheeks. Arrived.

"I'm going to open up this show with a song for my boy and his girl Blue." He smirked at the crowd. Toying with them, when I knew exactly where he was headed. "I think you'll all recognize it."

And there it was. The opening chords. The *early one morning, the sun was shining. I was laying in bed.*

People singing along. The cymbals rattling before the drums came in on the chorus.

And Blue was missing the whole goddamn thing.

The song was nearly six minutes long, but she wasn't back to me until it was through, and the next one, and Cheeks was on to originals. She came back with another amaretto sour, no doubt on my tab.

"You missed it," I told her.

She acted like she couldn't hear me, so I leaned in right into her ear and yelled it again, as loud as I could.

"Missed what?" she asked.

I told her.

"What?"

I told her again. *Tangled. up. in. blue.*

"Is that a song?"

I dumped what was left of my second beer over her head. Figured it was fair game after she tossed her drink in my face, and I only had a couple sips left.

"What's wrong with you?"

She was gone, pushing past people like nobody's business. Like in the old days when another girl would flirt me at the bar and Blue made no bones about getting in her face and telling her to step off because I was her man. Is there anything hotter? One night she even got in a fight with another girl. A Dominican with the kinkiest black hair, with blond highlights who face palmed her and tried to push her back, so Blue shoulder-tackled her back into the bar, hitting her own head against the edge in the process, and it looked like Blue only got madder for that impact, as if the other girl had hit her. Blue got her on the ground. When we got home, I let Blue get on top of me, a lot like that, full straddle and a flurry of motion, pulling at my hair.

Blue cut a path straight to the bathroom and shoved the door open with two hands. Reckless abandon. There were just two ladies' rooms, two men's rooms in the whole place, each with a single toilet and sink, almost always a line, and it was sheer luck for her to find one unlocked and unoccupied.

I followed after her.

The bathroom walls were covered in Sharpie scrawls and brown splotch liquor stains. The space was lit in fluorescent light, much brighter than the rest of the bar, and it smelled cleaner than you'd think, more like chemicals than piss, like somebody'd overdone it with bleach before opening. Blue ran the sink, the water glugging out in an uneven flow over her hands and she bent her head toward it as if she were figuring on whether she could fit her whole head under the faucet or if she'd have to cup her hands and pour it over herself to get at the beer suds in her hair.

I turned the lock behind me.

It wasn't just the lock to a bathroom door anymore. It was a lock to a time machine. Something unleashed via Cheeks' guitar and Blue's tank top and the beer. I took her upper arms in my hand and pushed her to the wall and kissed her as hard as I ever had. Harder. Until I could swear I tongued her uvula and she gagged for a second. Until I kissed her again and she bit my lip hard, flirting with the line between play and punishment and I knew that she had made this journey four, five years back through time with me.

I unbuttoned her jeans and pulled at the zipper, but it stuck. She tumbled over her jeans as I began to pull them down, more brute force than grace, all knotted up at her knees. I was on her.

I saw red. People talk about seeing red and mean they're angry. But this was more like passion. I saw Blue in a red cardigan, crying in my arms after she found out her grandmother kicked the bucket. Blue at the Italian restaurant behind a plate of zucchini-stuffed ravioli all smothered in marinara, where I asked if she would move in with me and she said yes and I felt like Superman because I could practically feel my life going somewhere *faster than a speeding locomotive.* And Blue's hair, all those red curls tumbling around me when she hugged me from behind, when she wore her red bikini with the pictures of seashells and sandcastles printed on it, when she rode on top of me and when I was on top of her in that moment. All that *red red red* dissolving into *Blue Blue Blue*.

Then the smash. The bright white flash. I was off her and thought I must've hit my head on the wall in my fervor. But there Blue was, on her knees, empty beer bottle in her hands that must have already been in the bathroom, the nearest weapon at hand. She let it fall to the ground. The guy in the bar had been right about how hard it was to break a beer bottle, because it didn't shatter on the floor, hadn't broken against my skull.

The moment crystallized. Blue hadn't been in that time machine at all and hadn't liked where I was heading. My head ached. I touched my fingers to my temple. She'd drawn blood. *Red red red.*

Blue Blue Blue.

The both of us straightened our clothes. I was still sitting on the floor when Blue wadded up a bunch of paper towel and ran them under cold water from the faucet before she touched them to where I was bleeding. It was as tender as we'd been in some time.

"It's not too bad," she said, and she was right, because it was more of an abrasion than a cut.

I washed my face with soap and water as somebody banged on the far side of the door and Blue told them to *mind your fucking business*. I didn't know how long we'd been in there, and anybody who'd seen me follow her in must have figured we were screwing. I guess I had some toilet paper sticking to the butt of my jeans. Blue took it off for me and we both laughed at that. Out of the bathroom, I bought her another amaretto sour without her asking.

We hung back by the bar, where it wasn't so crowded. Cheeks was playing another Dylan tune. I thought it was "Don't Think Twice, It's All Right," but by the time it got to the chorus, I realized I was wrong. This was a deeper cut. Maybe not Dylan at all, but a cover of someone else or something Cheeks had come up with on his own. Maybe not an old song at all, but some new frontier. Blue's hair still smelled like beer. I slid my arm around her waist and held her close.

TOMORROW IS A LONG TIME

Daren Dean

Cody suggested that they go to Slocum's funeral. He felt bad about it. He had never seen anyone die in front of him before except his grandma and she had died in a hospital bed from a stroke. It wasn't anything so violent as falling to your death. Cody couldn't help but feel responsible. It was his fault after all. Maybe if he hadn't started to walk toward the back door at just the moment the bees had come streaming out of the chimney, he could have warned the old man or steadied his ladder for him. Terri told him not to blame himself. His wife was very practical like that although he pointed out that she hadn't witnessed it as he had. It was a terrible image that seemed to play through his mind on a loop. The man lying there on the ground in an unnatural position with his neck and legs at such impossible angles, but she was right. It was just an accident and these things did happen unexpectedly.

Not only did she *not* want to go to the funeral but she was a little miffed that they still had to contend with bees coming out from behind a crack between the wall and the fireplace. She called them "killer bees" though they were just your garden variety honey bees. On the floor behind the window treatments and the furniture were dozens of dead bee bodies. She worried that Michaela would get stung or put the bees in her mouth. She was at the crawling backward stage now and she didn't know any better. Cody was soon discovering that babies put everything in their mouths that they could get their hands on. You had to watch a baby every second.

All Cody could do was look at his pretty wife with the dark brown eyes and put his hand on her smooth, tanned face and suggest they go out to Wrightsville Beach for a picnic with the baby. They drove to the beach on the crooked highway. Terri was so beautiful he felt love and a sharp twinge of pain in his chest that he would somehow lose her or that they might be separated one day. He couldn't explain this fear nor had he mentioned to her, but ever since the baby had come along he had felt this with a strong sense of dread. At the beach, they watched Michaela sitting and playing with her colorful plastic blocks on the blanket under the red umbrella that really wasn't made to withstand the sudden gusts of wind coming down the coast. He leaned on his arm near the baby to make sure she didn't eat too much sand.

He watched Terri in her white bikini soaking up the sun on a bright orange beach towel about twenty yards away, close to that expanse of beach where children played and people walked or jogged just above the lip of sand where the waves crashed onto the beach. She wanted to be near the water, but she would come back and sit with them under the umbrella after she had a chance to soak up the sun. Her skin was so smooth and tan. It was like tan velvet, he thought. When she turned over on her stomach he looked down the gap between her breasts, her firm and very pleasing backside, and her sun-dappled hair. The extra baby weight made her look even better. He thought about all the things he wanted to do with her later if the baby would cooperate by napping early. Terri looked up at him with her chin resting on the back of her hands at one point. She touched the bridge of her sunglasses and pulled them down with a finger and winked at him. He didn't think it was an exaggeration to imagine she could have been a model or at least one of the vixens in a music video. She was a little too thin before. He couldn't help but smile back at her.

A squadron of pelicans cast shadows over the beach. Cody glanced up to see the strange antediluvian air force. If Terri had been a little closer he would have told her how they reminded him of pterodactyls due to the shape of their wings and the way they flew in formation. They hadn't been to the beach in a while but there were always interesting sights to see. Like the bearded camera man taking photographs of surfers dangerously near the pier. About the same time, a wild looking middle-aged man appeared to be skiing up the beach with skis, pumping his arms vigorously as he landed the points of his poles into the sand to keep his dubious momentum going forward. People back home would have laughed to watch the skiing man trying to do something so defiantly ridiculous, but they would have shaken their collective head, *That's Wilmington for you!* Even though it was Wrightsville Beach, not Wilmington at all. The residents of the little beach community had bumper stickers that read *Tourists Go Home!*

Two teenage boys were walking along the beach and elbowing each other as they checked Terri out. He felt himself get a little mad but then he knew he would have done the same thing had he come upon such a beautiful woman on the beach. He looked up in time to watch a seahawk dive like a stone after fish in the surf not too far out. It was one of those lazy summer days where the sun sucked all the energy out of your body. He took a swig from a water bottle he had filled with white wine. The baby was laughing and smiling and it seemed like Cody could rest. He had the perfect child and the perfect wife.

A week later, Cody was sweeping up dead bee bodies with a broom into a blue plastic dustpan so that Terri wouldn't have to look at them and start complaining about how they had to move. He liked living in the little house but he wished he could talk her into moving into one of the little houses near Carolina Beach just a few streets from the waves of the Atlantic. He told her they would probably never get the chance to live so close to the beach ever again but she didn't want to be too far from the mall where she worked managing the Clinique makeup counter in Belk. He loved that she looked like an exquisite doctor or scientist devoted to the research of beauty in her requisite white lab coat.

A droning sound began to intrude on his thoughts until he realized it was coming from outside the house. It sounded like what he imagined a giant queen bee might sound if she were on the hunt for a new home. He went outside and heard the sound of the plane dangerously low overhead. It was a military plane, a bomber he thought, flying so low it seemed to rumble just over the tops of the long leaf pines and ancient live oaks of the neighborhood. He swore he could almost make out the face of the pilot and a uniformed spotter hanging halfway out of the side door. He didn't know enough about the military to tell which branch this plane belonged to, but it triggered a memory from the year before when they had driven down to Florida and arrived at the Pensacola lighthouse just in time to see the Navy's Blue Angels maneuver dramatically around the lighthouse before landing. The only thing dramatic about this plane was how low it was flying. Everyone in New Hanover county was waiting for the other shoe to drop. What would they bomb next? Uncertainty was in the air and the fear was palpable even as North Carolinians tried to go about life as usual.

Cody and Terri had moved to Wilmington from Bladen County just over two years earlier. She had just told him she was pregnant and they had decided together it was high time to get out on their own. He had always worked for his granddad and daddy on the tobacco farm doing anything that needed doing. The Robeson name was well known around Bladenboro, up in Dublin, and over in Elizabethtown. He had taken over his granddad's job picking up the Mexican laborers to work in the fields in the rusted Dodge when the old man's sight had become so questionable that he couldn't drive anymore. It was easy enough to do, but his daddy wouldn't give him much responsibility or much money and he was almost thirty years old. Too old to be treated like some snot-nosed kid.

It was true enough they had free rent since they lived in the converted tobacco barn outside the big house his parents lived in. He had helped his daddy turn the old barn into a little, oddly shaped apartment but he and Terri had never been able to get enough money together to buy their own place. She constantly talked about getting their own little piece of heaven. She didn't care if it was a trailer in Green Meadows Trailer Court just so long as it was theirs and they didn't have to constantly feel grateful or do favors for everyone in his family as payment. Besides, they hadn't been married very long and neither of them had embraced their in-laws although truth be known, they really weren't that different.

He took a job as a bartender for a dive called the Whipping Post that had a view of the Cape Fear river and was well-trafficked by a mix of locals, college students, and tourists. The owner was an eccentric who let him run the place as he saw fit and really seemed to not care much about the bar, alcohol, or even the customers as such. Instead, his nostalgia knew no bounds. Phil King seemed to travel a circuit around the Southeast buying old boats, tractor signs, Harleys, anything with an old west motif, ancient radios, jukeboxes, and 1950s Rock-N-Roll memorabilia. He seemed especially fond of anything relative to Elvis or Hank Williams. He was seemingly on a quest to fill the bar with all the leftover junk nobody in the southeast wanted anymore.

Cody didn't mind working there but Terri was worried he was going to fall in love with a drunken college student or some random female tourist. He tried to assure her wasn't interested in anyone but her. He wasn't exaggerating when he told her she was the most beautiful woman he had ever known but being pregnant made her feel fat and ugly. She got angry at him when he touched her belly. It was as if he couldn't do anything to suit her anymore and her suspicion that he was about to leave her and their unborn baby.

As the days went by Terri seemed to become more involved with her job and increasingly unhappy with him. Cody found this confusing since nothing had changed about how he felt about her. Now they were on different schedules so they saw each other less. Their lives seemed to be all about working and trading off taking care of the baby. She had just become the manager of the Clinique counter at Belk. She now made more money than he did, which made him feel like a failure but he decided not to tell her this since he didn't want her to feel bad. His daddy had told him the man was supposed to take care of his family and now it seemed like she was the one taking care of them. His daddy and Uncle Jesse took every opportunity to tell him he needed to keep his woman at home and in line but he didn't know how to tell them he didn't think like they did. He wanted the best for Terri and if that meant she did better at work, then so be it. He stayed silent on the issue in front of the men.

The busy time for both of them was now the weekend and they had to start paying an older woman down the street named Deloris to watch the baby while they were at work. It felt like lives on different schedules were beginning to take their toll. At just six weeks old, they had had to take the baby to daycare during the week so Terri could go back to work. They both felt really awful about handing their baby over to strangers but not working wasn't an option in Terri's mind. She was their little jewel and they just handed her off to a skinny lady with gray hair streaked with blonde highlights who called herself Ms. Joy. Out in the truck, Terri leaned across the seat and grabbed his shirt collar and cried with her face pressed against him. He could feel her hot tears dampening his chest. When she was finished she sat back in the seat and looked at him with a long face, smeared mascara blotched around those dark brown eyes. She thought more than she said. He smiled at her and she laughed in embarrassment although there was nothing to be embarrassed about as they put their heads together across the console.

"Should I go back in and get her?"

"Take me to work," She shook her head and dabbed her eyes with tissue. She flipped down the sunvisor because it had a mirror on the other side, took out her makeup bag, and went to work on "fixing" her face. It didn't need fixing he wanted to say, should have said, since he loved her for being so tender hearted.

Phil asked him to take on more responsibility at the bar. He had been promoted to head bartender and received a much-needed raise. It meant he had to come in earlier in the afternoon to run the bar, do the prep and scheduling. Some nights he felt good about his job and almost like a celebrity. People knew his name and one night he had even received a fifty-dollar tip from a businessman who had only had one drink.

A middle-aged woman in a black cocktail dress came out while he was on a smoke break in the alley and suddenly lunged at him, planting a drunken lip-lock on him and awkwardly groped him. He grabbed her hand and held her at arm's length. He was at heart just a simple man trying to do his job and hadn't bargained for the irrational things people did when they were under the influence. She was what his granddad could have called a handsome woman. It was easy to see she had once been very beautiful and not so long ago. If he had seen her ten years ago, she probably could have had any man she wanted. In fact, she probably still could now if she was sober. Before he could say anything she stumbled awkwardly on the bricks, one of her pointed heels had become lodged between the alley's bricks and when she tried to yank it out, it snapped off at the heel.

She sneered drunkenly at him, "Do you realize how expensive these heels are? They cost more than you make in a night!" Before he could think of something to say back to her she spat out, "What are you . . . gay or something?" She tottered on one high heel and did a peg leg walk back into the bar to her husband who looked wealthy, important. He hoped they left before he had to go back in since Donnie couldn't run the place alone, not on a Saturday night.

Still, his promotion seemed like a good thing and they had dinner at the Pilot House restaurant to celebrate. Now they were both managers and they really needed the money more than ever to afford Michaela's daycare and her increasing doctor's visits. The baby had been getting sick recently and her little body heaved and retched so much they were both terrified that she might die. She was so tiny, a long and skinny baby. "Bowtie man" (what they called one of the rotating doctors at their pediatrician's office) typed furiously into his Blackberry and finally came up with rotavirus as the culprit but somehow this didn't seem right. The bees hadn't gone away either but he continued to try to clean them up so Terri wouldn't get too upset.

Terri said she wanted to go back to Bladen County because she missed her family. The Smiths were good people and he couldn't help feeling bad about taking their daughter away from them since he knew they all loved her so. He felt, no knew, he hadn't done right by them in more ways than one. Wilmington was just too big and fast for her, she said. Her beautiful dark eyes filled with tears and she wept at the kitchen table until Michaela pulled herself up on Cody's leg said her first word, not Mama or Dada, but *kitty*. Terri scooped the baby up in her arms. They both laughed at that, couldn't help it, since they had each been trying to convince her to say mama or daddy when the other one wasn't around. Cody thought his wife would get over her homesickness eventually. It was just a passing phase and perfectly normal he told her. She didn't say anything and took the dinner dishes into the kitchen to clean up. They could go visiting on the weekend he said, but he couldn't bring himself to go back and face the judgmental eyes of his granddad that regarded working in a bar as a sinful occupation. His daddy just thought he was wasting his life. His elders both expected him to assume his position running the farm even though they both knew an operation like theirs was too small to make it anymore. They were a dying breed.

On Michaela's first birthday Terri made a homemade birthday cake. They lit a single candle and sang happy birthday to her and she seemed delighted when they helped her blow out the candle. The baby put both hands into the cake and pulled out fistfulls before cramming it into her mouth. He couldn't remember ever being happier except at the moment of her birth. Even on his wedding day he had been more terrified than happy due. In the moment, he had been struck by the idea he was doing this thing adults do, but the birth of the baby had been pure joy. Michaela did a face plant in the center of the cake and when she raised her head cake stuck to her cheeks and forehead, a big dollop of white icing on her nose, and a big smile behind the cake. Terri leaned her head on his shoulder and he didn't feel like an impostor as a husband or a dad in that moment.

It was a Saturday afternoon and he was feeling under the weather at home with the baby when he saw a figure in full camo gear run by his dining room window carrying an assault rifle. One eye checked to see that Michaela was bopping up and down in her playpen, while the other eye forced him to stumble toward the window to see what was going on. At first, he thought it had something to do with 9/11. Was al-Qaeda literally in his backyard? And why did President Bush want to send troops to Iraq instead of Afghanistan? The side road was blocked off by Wilmington police cars so he couldn't take the baby anywhere since the driveway was effectively blocked off. The figure in full camo and hood was leaning into the deep ditch like it was a World War I trench. He was aiming through the trees, past his neighbor's backyard, and aiming his rifle toward something or someone, but the only window on that side of the house was obscured by his neighbor's fence line.

The need to protect the baby welled up within him so much so that he felt tears stinging his eyes at the mere idea that something might happen to his precious daughter. He imagined himself packing a bag for the baby, putting it into her stroller, and maybe taking her to Salt Works just a couple of blocks away and have some pancakes for breakfast until the sting or whatever it was blew over. Whoever the police were after might also have guns.

What if a stray bullet hit one of them even here in the house? He had heard of this happening many times over the years. It wasn't uncommon at all.

There was the squawking sound of a male voice through a bullhorn outside. The sound of the voice was distorted and it echoed so it was impossible to distinguish individual words. The voice made him angry. It had even sent the crows that liked to strut around in the medium across the street where it was said Wilmington had once had a trolley car system running back in the 1920s but if that was right the tracks were long gone. By the sounds outside, the police had someone cornered their quarry a couple of blocks north of the house. Cody knew there was an apartment complex in that area but it was also not far from College avenue, which was a very busy road lined with businesses and homes the further north you went.

The sniper in his ditch must have fired his weapon. He strode over to the window and by pushing the filmy white curtains aside and pressing his forehead against the window he could just makeout the sniper who had jumped out of the ditch with his rifle and was now running across his backyard and out of sight. Cody went to the baby's room, plucked the baby out of her playpen though he knew she needed a change since she was beginning to whine at her discomfort, buckled her into her baby seat, shut the bedroom door, and sat down on the floor with her in the middle of their little house in the small dining room to wait for it to end. Terri had pumped some breast milk and he went to the fridge and pulled out a bottle for the baby to keep her pacified for the time being while he quickly changed her.

Suddenly, there was a barrage of gunfire outside. Instinctively he fell flat on the floor and positioned his body so that he was almost on top of the baby to protect her if a stray bullet happened to come in their direction. He imagined, though not because he wanted to, trying to explain to Terri that the baby had been shot by a stray bullet from the police or whoever it was they were after and he shook his head no to make the thought leave his mind. He feared imagining the event might make it happen or will it into existence.

"No!" he said out loud. "I don't want that to happen." Sometimes he imagined things like this and they seemed so real it was as if they had happened in that instant.

The barrage went silent. It was almost eerily quiet. It seemed to be indicative of the police had caught their man or men. He wondered if the local news would have anything to report about it later that evening. The cop cars had vanished from his street almost as if they had never been there. He picked up the house phone and called Terri to tell her what had happened. "Oh my god!" she shrieked. Her distress was like someone was stabbing him in the heart with an icepick. She was going to ask to take off early and come home. She wanted to be with the baby, with him.

It was more than twenty minutes he heard her little Dodge Colt crunching the pea gravel in the driveway. He met her at the door with the baby who squealed with delight as they locked in a three-way embrace in the kitchen. Even though the dishes needed to be done and the laundry was piling up, they were reunited in safety for the moment. Terri was weeping with a mixture of fear and relief. *Daddy-Mommy,* Michaela said. This made them laugh. The baby squealed again and declared, *eat, eat, eat!* Cody felt closer to them than ever, but he feared it would never last. The good things in life were fleeting.

He was picking up the big pine cones from the long leaf pines out in the yard with a gloved hand and putting the pointy objects into a black trash bag that didn't want to stay open. The pine cones were so large you had to pick them up or they would seriously damage or bend the mower's blade over time. A fairly good-sized pile of pine straw had managed to accumulate by the road in the front yard and three people had already stopped by to ask if they could "take it off his hands" but that just meant they didn't want to pay for it. He was going to use it around the house as edging. Terri had taken the baby back to Bladenboro to live with her mama. He had started drinking while he was working at the bar, and she didn't like it. She had grown up, as they both had, in the Baptist church. Being a bartender was bad enough in her eyes, but drinking on the job had put him on the road to ruin. He had tried to point out it wasn't as if she were a tea totaler herself or something, but the accusation felt hollow and argumentative on his part. She was convinced he didn't care about her or the baby and said the demon of drink was at his elbow all weekend at the Whipping Post. It didn't sound like her. It sounded like her mother speaking through her like in an article he had once read about a mesmerism and seances that were popular back in the early twentieth century, except his mother-in-law was relentlessly still alive and haunted him like a specter in the physical world. Terri's teary red eyes and trembling lips angered him and made him want to kiss her at the same time.

Cody thought if he fixed the place up for her she would see he did care about her and the baby. After a few days without the two of them it was clear his life wasn't worth a plug-nickel, which was something his granddad liked to say and now here he was, a modern person in a new century, saying things tobacco farmers said. Even the words proceeding out of his mouth called his blood and body home. His wife and family were all back in Bladen county trying to pull him back there, but he felt he had one foot back home and one foot firmly planted anywhere-but-there. Folks back home considered New Hanover county "the big city" where all the people with lacks morals dwelled. It was funny to hear them refer to it as the big city or his daddy simply called it Babylon. He loved the people back home, but he sometimes laughed at them even though they weren't joining in. He didn't want them to be backward and judgmental like they were. He considered himself open-minded and modern. He loved them, but he hated their small-mindedness toward people who were different or outsiders to their small world in southern North Carolina. It disturbed him that he had grown up with them, but was now out of step with his own.

What he needed to do was make the place into a garden for Terri and the baby. When he went by the electric coop to pay his rent he was telling the secretary, Deborah, about how Terri had left and his idea to plant a garden for her in the big backyard. Mr. Driscoll came out of his office and told him he thought a garden was a fine idea and gave him suggestions about what to grow. He favored corn, squash, and tomato plants.

Monday was his regular day off. His neighbor, Dan, across the street allowed him to use his tiller and the next thing he knew he was tilling an area in the backyard near the fence-line while the crows squawked at him from the trees. It felt good to be doing something outside and physical again instead of in a dark bar where the floorboards reeked with the odor of spilled beers and the warm humid nights seem to usher in the skunk scent of urine from the street. The sun warmed his skin and he felt that he was where he belonged for now but always in the back of his mind a feeling of disquiet. But today was going to be a good one.

The dogwood in his side yard was beginning to bloom with its impressive white flowers. He wished Terri were here to see it with him even though this time of year usually bothered her allergies. He took off his shirt and tucked part of it in his jeans and let most of it hang out to his side. He was beginning to work up a sweat, but he had picked up a large Gatorade and a pack of Marlboro Light 100's at Snuggers, a small convenience store, a couple of blocks away. Since he had started working at the bar he had taken to smoking and ever since Terri left him he didn't have to hide it. It reminded him that the last garden he had tilled was for his grandma. Just thinking about how she would sit in the shade of the big live oak by the old curing barn and watch him work like she was watching the best soap opera ever made him feel good, but then he couldn't help thinking she was gone now. Somehow that loss was now mixed up with the loss of his wife and daughter and he really didn't know what to do. He did not want to give in to Terri, but he also wanted them both back. He didn't want anyone to think he was so weak. His granddad always told him what he was beginning to suspect was a myth of what real men did. The garden was for them he told himself as he started pushing the tiller again. He might plant some watermelon for Michaela. He could see her eating watermelon on a warm southern night on the steps of the back porch spitting seeds and watermelon juice all over face and clothes. She was such a messy little eater.

A neighbor drove by and waved at him with a big smile on her face. He waved back. People loved to watch a person work, he thought.

The baby had turned their world upside down. At least, he was thinking this as he was cleaning up forgotten dirty glasses from the night before in the back bar. He squeezed out a white rag from a little plastic bucket with a mixture of a little too much bleach and warm water before he began to wide down the bar. Now that Terri and the baby were gone all he had were memories now. As he remembered it, even his Granddad had stopped talking about the Four Horseman of the Apocalypse and the Last Days long enough to ride with Cody's Mom and Dad to New Hanover County Hospital and see their new baby. The old man looked at her and pronounced her beautiful and precious and the tender side of the tobacco farmer emerged like a cicada after thirteen years.

But then they had ruined it by telling him how he needed to bring Terri and the baby back to Bladen

County to be with family. They all missed them, they said. He felt their love, their collective influence, like a strait jacket. He just nodded. They were his elders and he didn't have the heart to tell them he wasn't coming back. At least, not right now. He was enjoying his independence. He was even saving up to buy a little place at Carolina Beach. Ever since his buddy Dave from back home had taken him four-wheeling and surf-fishing on the beach along the southern peninsula he had decided he would live there before he moved away. At least, that was his plan but he hadn't wanted to do it alone.

It hadn't dawned on him that she was angry with him. At least, not at the time. They were still newlyweds then. He did remember that. She wouldn't allow herself to say why she was peeved and retreated into silence that left him chastened, and he could feel her anger palpable and alive. They had been talking about how they needed a new car and he had driven up to Jacksonville's Air Force base to buy a used pickup with their savings, what little of it they had then, and without discussing it with her first.

That was the part that had hurt Terri's feelings and then made her so angry she could barely speak to him. It had "riled" her was what his granddad had said about it. It was an old blue and white Chevy C10. The kind of truck his dad had driven back when he was a kid. The nostalgia of settling in behind the wheel had put him in an arm bar and forced him to count out the bills out of the skinny white envelope the bank had given him when he had withdrawn the money from savings.

Now, she was angry again and it had finally dawned on him that this was another time (one of many) he had failed to take her feelings into consideration. He just couldn't understand her need for her own family when he was so done, at least for now, with feeling obligations toward his own. If they needed anything, he would bend over backwards for them in a pinch, but he was just tired of listening to their advice. He had to find his own way. Whatever he did today was what he would be doing tomorrow and farming was for a dying a breed in his book. The government wouldn't allow the small farmer to make it anymore. Besides all that, Terri needed help with the baby too. Not a man's help, not with a baby, he was sure she would say if she allowed herself to say anything at all.

He had called her one lonely Monday night at her parent's house and he was still relieved to hear that she was calculating the baby's age in months. He wished there were a way to make everything up to her without having to give in and move back to the farm. As a man, he didn't want to lose face in that way. He feared, too, that if he gave in she would lose respect for him even though she had got what she wanted. The heart of a woman was difficult to plumb to its depths. He knew a man could never hold his breath long enough to reach the emotional channels a woman owned.

All this time he was still sweeping up the little bee bodies in the dustbin. Not as many recently since the weather had begun to turn to fall. One night he woke from a disturbing dream of Michaela crawling around on the hardwood floor in the living room eating the little bee bodies like raisins. He couldn't believe they weren't stinging her mouth. As she ate, she began to transform. Her body grew darker. Little antennae sprouted on her forehead and began to grow. She started scuffling in circles around the floor faster and faster like an insect herself until she sprouted bee wings from the back of her little onesie and began buzzing and flying around the room, smashing into the lamps, knocking over the television in the corner, and bumping against the windows to be let out. Finally, she managed to bump into the screen door a couple of times and flew out of the house as he stood there in slack-jawed amazement. "Terri! Terri! Come quick! The baby just flew out of the house!" He ran after her, but she flew too fast for him. She was really buzzing loudly like a hive and heading south out of Wilmington. How would he explain to Terri that he had allowed Michaela to eat the bees off the floor and now she had buzzed away? When he awoke his dream anxiety turned back to reality. Terri and Michaela had both flown away.

Cody's sister Amber called from back home to tell him their brother Craig was killed by an IED in Baghdad. He was so surprised by the news he dropped the phone and had to bend down and pick it back up off the floor. He could hear her weeping over the phone as she tried to tell him about the men in uniform who had come to the door and how Daddy knew as soon as they pulled up in the driveway what they were going to say. Cody's mind was racing and he couldn't concentrate on what she was saying anymore. The words were spilling out and he wanted time, the words, to go back in reverse into her mouth. He could hang up the phone again. He wanted to go back to his old worries and not have this new, terrible thing hanging over his head like a black anvil.

Craig must have been about fifteen and now deeply tanned from working his summer job bucking bales of hay with their cousins on their uncle's spread. His brother had grown suddenly muscular from lifting weights. A stubble of wiry beard was on his face. He had transformed into a man overnight in Cody's eyes. It was incredible to him because he had been his older brother, an older kid he worshipped, but now he had almost reached godlike status although he would never have said such an embarrassing thing out loud. There was no denying it. Craig was cool.

It was a Sunday morning about 5am when Craig touched his shoulder. "You want to come with me CC?" His brother stood over his bed and through sleepy eyes Cody could see that he held his Marlin by the stock.

"You going hunting?"

Craig's eyes cut away as if someone were watching him from the corner of the room. "You coming or not?"

"Okay," Cody said. "Where we going? What season is it?"

"No season you ever heard of. To the mountain. Let's go." His brother had a pack of cigarettes bulging from the shoulder of his shirt sleeve. He smoked Marlboro Light 100s. He loved his big brother because he was nice to him and he was tough.

He knew the exact spot he was talking about when he said that. It would take a little while to get there and it was on someone else's property. They would have to cross three barbed wire fences. Neither of them knew whose land it was. They could have asked their daddy, but he would have lectured them about private property. In one deft movement he flipped the sheet back and sat up on the bed. He put on his jeans, a t-shirt with the number 12 on it, and a pair of holey Converse.

"I'm wearing my holy shoes today," he said. Normally Craig would laugh at that, but he gave a curt nod.

They ate cold pulled pork on Wonder bread for breakfast. It was still good, but he would have liked it better warm but he could tell Craig was in a hurry to get out of the house.

The boys had stayed up all night with their daddy and Uncle Jesse at the pig pickin' the previous weekend after everyone else had gone to bed. The men took turns telling tall tales they swore were true about the Beast of Bladenboro; a folk creature equal parts mountain lion and vampire from all the stories. Cody believed them all. Friends and family from all over the state would descend on the place the next day and they would all know the men had stayed up to slow cook the meat. Wonder of wonders, they had even allowed Craig to smoke in front of them and drink a beer since he was as big as a man now. The men only did things they normally said were wrong like letting kids smoke and drink when their wives weren't around.

"You're not old enough yet." Daddy said.

"When will I be old enough?" Cody asked.

"One day," Daddy said. "We'll both know it, but that time ain't now."

"The boy is too much of a pussy," Granddad said. "You and Maureen treat him like a baby on the tit."

Luckily it was dark and nobody could see Cody's face flush. Sometimes the men said things about him as if he weren't sitting right there in front of him. His eyes filled with his tears that his Granddad thought he wasn't tough enough. The men talked about being tough all the time. His daddy and Granddad had been known for their bad tempers and reputations as men not to mess with. His daddy's fist was like a hamhock it was so big. Uncle Jesse once told him he had women's hands just matter-of-factly. It all served to make him want to do something they would all know only a tough kid, a tough man, could do.

Later Granddad was asleep in his lawn chair and snoring quietly in front of the campfire. Cody pointed at him. Daddy put a finger up to his lips. They had all laughed quietly, trying mightily not to make a sound. It was funny, but Cody wasn't sure why but it was. Granddad was old and couldn't stay awake so late. Whoever could hack it and stay awake the longest had bragging rights the next day.

Uncle Jesse noticed him pouting about being called a pussy and when his daddy wasn't looking his uncle gave him an ink pen to look at in the fire light that showed a woman's clothes disappearing when you flipped it upside down and back again. "You will be an old man like me before you know it."

"How old are you, Uncle Jesse?"

"How old do you think?"

"I don't know," he said. "About forty?"

"Damn kid," Uncle Jesse said. "I'm twenty-nine. Where'd you get forty?"

"Well, I don't know. You're always saying how old you are. I figured you was really old."

"Christ," Uncle Jesse shook his head. "I'm going to go get another bottle of Miller and I ain't letting you drink one with me until you're twenty-one."

"I don't like beer anyway," he stared at the tiny woman as her clothes magically appeared again. "It tastes like horse piss."

"Well," Uncle Jesse said. "If you're anything like the rest of us. And it looks like you are. You will like it well enough when you're older."

"Why does everyone always say that?" Cody asked. "You will understand when you're older."

"You know," he said. "You're right. By the time you're old enough to understand anything, the few things you do learn come too late to help you very much." He took the pen back and stuck in his shirt pocket like he might have to make a grocery list later. He would remember that night forever. It was the first time he stayed up all night with the men without falling asleep. He remembered watching the flames of their campfire. The flames reached up to the moon like savage prayers. The wood and ashes popping like magic into the starry night sky of midnight blue. But he never could summon up very many memories of the family get-together the next day.

The dawn was orange and splotched across the eastern sky like a Rorschach test. The big live oaks in the back allowed the color in through the veil of Spanish moss. Sergeant, their big German shepherd-yellow lab mix, met them at the backdoor and had to poke his big nose with the pink tip into their hands before he allowed them to get through the back door.

"Don't let the screen door slam shut," Craig hissed. He handed Cody his nice Case knife, it was red like a man's blood, with a serious expression that told him to hang onto it and don't lose it! Cody slid the knife into the front pocket of his jeans.

Cody took his daddy's old Marlin out of the gun case. If he noticed it missing, and he probably wouldn't, he would likely get his ass handed to him. Craig gave him a look that asked, are you sure about that? Cody gave him a big grin.

"Your funeral, bro," Craig whispered.

Cody put on a hunting vest like Craig wore to hold a box of ammo in the zipper pocket.

After they passed the woodpile, Craig broke into a jog even though he was wearing heavy work boots. His hair was long and down to his shoulders. He was running cross country at school as a Sophmore and had made varsity when he was a Freshman. Cody thought he might run cross country when he was in high school too. He would be a freshman when Cody was a senior. It would be cool to be on the same team with him. The sound Cody was most aware of was the rhythmic sound of the ammo in his pocket with each stride.

They passed through the hayfield running the old dog trots as they passed the haystacks. They came to a rust-colored cattle gate and climbed over it instead of unwinding the chain and opening it up. It was more fun this way although it made Granddad mad. The Herefords looked at them like they were crazy as they jogged across the field. Cody pretended they were Seneca. He was reading the second book in a series called "The White Indian" by Donald Clayton Porter and it was about the Seneca and how they ran like marathon runners whenever they were on the warpath with other Iroquois tribes. The only Indians around he had ever heard about were the Lumbee Indians.

Cody was beginning to feel a stitch in his side, but he pushed himself. He didn't want to lose sight of

Craig even though he knew exactly where he was going. Craig was pulling ahead now. He ran like a coyote into the brush. Man, Cody whispered to himself. His brother had disappeared into a knotted copse of pine. He smiled to himself because he took an oblique angle that he thought might get him to their spot first. The Marlin was getting heavy so he switched it to the other hand as he leapt up on an oak that had been felled by Mother Nature. It looked like it was taking a nap and landed in such a way that it was like a bridge over the fence it covered. The tree limbs had spiked into the ground and kept it from crushing the barbed wire fence. Nobody but him and his brother had been back through there in ages. He balanced himself with the Marlin like he was doing a tightrope act for the squirrels as he used the trunk of the oak as a footbridge. When he jumped down he began to run hard now, dodging the young saplings, cedars, and hickory. It was his mission to beat Craig to their spot.

When he arrived at the spot, chest heaving and out of breath, Craig was already leaning against a great rocky outcropping of the creek bank. Craig looked at him over his shoulder and motioned to him to be quiet as he approached. His Browning already leaned against a tree. His brother's attention was on something down in the creek below. When Cody approached close enough to peer over the ridge Craig pointed to a wood ibis, just over three foot tall, strutted around in the water with a dignified air about it. Cody put the Marlin to his shoulder, sighted the ibis, and just as he squeezed the trigger Craig grabbed the barrel and pushed it way from the bird as the rifle barked. The startled bird took a few clumsy, halting steps like a drunk stepping in post holes before it threw himself into the tar heel sky. The single gunshot echoed across the pocosin.

"What did you do that for?" Cody hollered.

Craig cocked his head to look at his brother, "What the hell's wrong with you! You don't go just shooting anything that moves because you've got a gun. Give me that." He yanked the Marlin away from Cody. His brother's face red, hands trembling with a rage he could not account for. Their daddy blamed teenaged hormones raging. He leaned the Marlin against the same tree as his Browning where they sat like witnesses for the prosecution.

"I'm sorry," Cody said. He was shocked and confused. Isn't shooting what they had come to do? "I didn't know . . . it's not my fault."

"It's not your fault?" Craig said. "What are you even talking about?"

Cody shrugged, "I don't know."

Now in his mind that single shot continued to echo grievously down through the years of his life.

It was a Sunday when they heard the news. He was sandwiched in between his Granddad and Craig in the GMC heading into town. The old man liked to listen to the radio, especially the farm report, with the volume blasting. When the announcer told the story of the Sheriff's department investigation into a mysterious shooting of a Bladenboro first grader who had been mysteriously murdered in her home. Cody didn't think too much of it at first since he rarely paid any attention to the news but when they revealed that it was the Smith family's little girl, Angela, he felt something like a dagger in the pit of his stomach. All the kids on Cody's school bus called her Angel. She was a cute little girl, hard to forget, that the older girls petted and fawned over her ash-blonde hair and blue eyes. She was almost the photo-negative of her darker complected older sister.

Just at that moment, his granddad bumped his knee with the knob of the gear shift as he downshifted for a steep hill. It felt like an accusation, so he looked quickly at the old man who calmly kept his eyes on the road and gave Cody's leg a little reassuring tap. A dreamy smile played on the old man's lips as if he hadn't been listening to the blaring radio. The windshield was muddy with dirt from the field. The old man ran the windshield and pumped washer fluid to clean it at the same time. Craig dug his ribs hard and shot Cody his mean eyes. It was an expression he had learned from their daddy. Cody could see he would look just like their daddy when he grew up, he could see every judgmental bone in his face. It was an expression that held an accusation of wrongdoing and maybe even punishment.

What? He mouthed soundlessly to Craig.

That little girl . . . he mouthed back slowly and glanced at their granddad. Craig had his elbow positioned up on the lip of the passenger door where the window began. He had his thumb pressed to his cheek and his finger pushed hard against his temple.

Cody shook his head. He wasn't following his brother's meaning at first.

You! Craig held his hand out and made a shooting hand gesture and motioned with his head for emphasis.

Cody felt his heart leap in his chest. Could it be? That little girl was dead because of what had happened on "the mountain" when he tried to shoot the ibis? He couldn't believe it; he didn't want to believe it. He pictured Angel getting on the bus with her sister Terri, leading her by the hand, down the aisle to sit next to her in one of the dark green bus seats. He could see her repositioning herself in the seat because of her impossibly large backpack and her pink-little-pure lunchbox. The low rumbling of the bus as it labored down the gravel road and vibrated his entire body. He noted her cute angel face and honey-blonde hair as she turned to say *hi* to another little girl her age sitting across the aisle. And it could have been a moment later, or several days later, Terri sat sideways in the bus seat next to Angel and struck him with a sudden smile. A moody girl, bright and dark, wearing black hand-me-down clothes but possessed of an undeniable, striking beauty.

He wanted to scream or cry, but he forced all the emotion down as he sat in the truck. What had he done? How could something so freakish happen? He couldn't have shot someone in that house from such a distance if he had tried. It couldn't be done. Even Craig couldn't have made such a shot even after his military training; a marksman on the shooting range. It was unthinkable. And yet it had happened. He knew it but he also knew he would never, could never, tell anyone. It would have to be a secret he kept until his grave as much as the good angel on his shoulder wanted him to confess. It remained just another tragic mystery in Bladen County over the years.

When he was a sophomore in high school he started dating Terri Smith almost as an act of absolution though he wouldn't have put it that way at the time. He hoped he could somehow be forgiven without ever admitting his guilt, but what he had done, and failed to admit, ate him up from the inside. The guilt convinced him he wasn't completely lost. He convinced himself that he loved her, and then he did, but their relationship had a taint to it that only he knew the depths of it though she sensed it. If he was sometimes distant; she, for her part, chalked it up the fact that he was a Robeson and that's how the Robeson men were. They were known for their moodiness and sometimes violent outbursts.

Once he began dating her, Craig stopped talking to him almost completely. Cody knew Craig was afraid he would tell what had happened all those years ago. When they were together his brother wouldn't even acknowledge their existence. Cody felt like he had lost a brother just as much as Terri had lost a sister. It wasn't long after that his brother enlisted in the Army and was sent overseas. He had sent Craig several letters and they had all been returned unopened. His daddy gave him updates about Craig like he was a boy he had once gone to school with. He knew there was a rift between the brothers, but he had never asked about it because he felt it was a personal matter between them to resolve or not. And how his brother was dead and there was no time left for reconciliation.

The bees had been dormant through an especially cold winter. It had even snowed. It was a rare event in Wilmington. Cody had seen his neighbors outside taking pictures of each other in the snow. The public schools, colleges, and churches had all canceled due to the slick, dangerous conditions.

This meant everyone went to the grocery stores and the Independence mall to shop out of sheer boredom. Cody had the day off from the Whipping Post and was preparing for the return of Terri and Michaela. The Baptist preacher at the church she went to convinced her that a woman's place was by her husband's side no matter what or so she said. He didn't care either way he just wanted his family back. He needed them both. Still, he made sure there were no remnant bee bodies hiding in the corners as evidence.

He spotted the car before it had even turned off his street. He was smoking on the screened-in porch, but he nervously stubbed it out and tossed the smoldering butt into the Maxwell House coffee can he kept in the corner for just that purpose. The day was bright and sunny with bright cotton cumulus clouds on a cerulean backdrop. The sun highlighted Michaela's strawberry-blonde hair as she stood holding her mother's hand in the gravel driveway. The iridescent white blossoms of the flowering dogwood in the yard seemed to preside over the moment.

"Daddy!" Michaela squealed. "Daddy! Daddy!" Her little arms flew up over her head and her face beamed with excitement. She was wearing a satin, pearl white, church dress with white leggings and glossy black shoes.

He felt his heart might burst with tenderness and love. She was so tiny and it seemed odd to see a person so little walking around in the world and yet his love for her was outsized. It made him want to protect her from all the bad in the world. With his eyes brimming with tears, he closed the space between them and lifted her in the air and spun her in circles. The sun glinted so that one instant he could see her little pixie face and the next it was obscured in shadow and then revealed again as they continued to whirl in the grass and pine straw in the yard. He could feel her heart pounding against the palm of his hand as they spun.

After they stopped spinning, Terri came to them and Cody buried his nose in the bouquet of her hair and he felt whole that he had his family back. If they could just make it until tomorrow as a family he felt everything would be all right. He held his toddler against him on one hip and his wife next to him on the other. The tears fell in rivulets down his face. Terri ducked her head and stared into his eyes, but he didn't want her to see his pain. He was theirs and they were complete as long as he never spoke of that long ago day.

LUCKY DAY

Patricia Q. Bidar

I'm a lucky bastard of scattered habits. My books marked by ladies' underthings. They bring me tea and flowers and leave earrings in my bedclothes.

She is the best of them, honey hair and citrine eyes I daren't meet. At eight in the morning, I awake in a jumble of sheets. Slip out in the nick of time. Husbandly shouts emit like brass notes from between window rails. The scent of her is still on my hands.

At ten o'clock I hear from friends: she's divorced. If I have something to do with that, no one but me and honey-headed her could connect the dots. We are immaculate.

I hear she's fled: Ibiza. At noon I carry on in gray Astoria, under the 1964 bridge to Washington State. By two, I'm in Rock Springs, Wyoming. Riding to the trona mines with dirty-necked men in a busted down truck.

Four p.m. finds me on the downswing, an ordinary rector at a Rust Belt house of prayer. When I finish, the pews shine amber.

By six, I'm running sound at the Fort Worth opera house. When the lights dim, I feel a tug on my laces.

I know not to meet those olive-lemon eyes. She extends an invitation in Catalan. In a low postscript, she calls me a fraudulent work of art.

She performs her warbling singthing to wild acclaim. But before the curtain, she's gone. I rise from my soundboard. My knotted-together laces piledrive me to carpet. I loosen my tie and reach for my comb.

Ten p.m. finds me walking the highway, graceless and bleary. Music caroms in my head. A black splash strikes my legs. Her and those eyes: that lethal duo. I meet citrine and come to rest without regret.

I awake at midnight, ensnared and alone. Beyond the floating drape splays Lake Pontchartrain, that talismanic ten-mile bridge. It would appear my luck is gone. I'm unensnared; face down in estuary mud.

BOB DYLAN'S ADDRESS TO THE DEL RIO, TEXAS CHAMBER OF COMMERCE

John Waddy Bullion

I once called this town "one of the United States, one of the bigger ones", and people would ask me, "what does that mean?" I am here to tell you it doesn't mean a thing. I said what I said about this place. But just because I said something about something doesn't mean that it means anything. And even though I always say what I mean, it's impossible to explain what I mean. If I came into your town and saw the junkys caressing fire into their arms behind your bus station and I said, "this is a drug town", you would say, and rightfully so, that's a lot of rubbish. This is not a drug town. Even if it is, it isn't.

I wrote a song about this town once. Except of course it wasn't about this town at all. It was about my friend, the painter, who lives here. Except he doesn't live here, not year-round anyway. He splits his time between this place and Mexico City, which is another one of the ones, one of the bigger ones. My friend the painter is also one of the ones, but he is one of the only ones. He knows the long story behind this town. I wrote that song so that I could trade places with him. And he drew a self-portrait so that he could trade places with me. Now he owns a chain of grocery stores. It used to be one way, and now it's another. Rightfully so.

TERMINAL BLUE

Amy Bassin & Mark Blickley

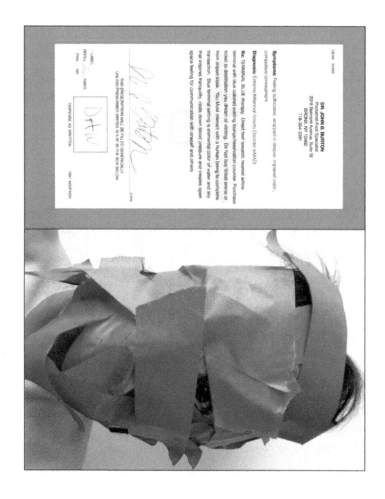

EL BORRACHO

Mark Rogers

Afternoon sunlight slanted through the high, glass tile windows of El Chupacabra, a cantina on Mexicali's Avenida del Cabildo. The sunlight raked the bar top's plywood surface, throwing flecks of cigarette ash into high relief. A TV on a shelf played *El Gordo y La Flaca* with the sound on mute. The fat man laughed as the skinny woman twirled her hand in the air.

The floor of the bar was scuffed black and white checkerboard tiles. There was space for only three tiny tables with chairs. That didn't matter—almost all the patrons preferred to sit at the bar.

The plaster wall opposite the bar top was blank.

Rodrigo—El Chupacabra's owner and sole bartender—stared at this blank wall during lulls in business, which were plentiful. Rodrigo had only made it through sixth grade, but a phrase from a week studying Egypt had stayed with him: *Horror vacui.* The concept that nature (and Egyptians) abhorred an empty space.

A sole masonry nail protruded from the wall, dating back to the day Rodrigo attempted to fill the empty space with an oversized calendar sold by a peddler. The calendar was primarily a rousing illustration of an Aztec warrior in a feathered headdress and cloak, standing next to a fallen Aztec maiden. The warrior pulls back on a bow, preparing to release an arrow at the sun. It was a stirring image—the maiden's curves were shown to full advantage.

For a week, Rodrigo enjoyed staring at the calendar. There was a problem, though. His customers didn't come to El Chupacabra to contemplate the passing of time. They came to erase time's passage. Glancing over their shoulders at the calendar, they saw the date, not the maiden. It reminded them of all the things they were neglecting and all the things that awaited them once they put the bottle down.

The calendar was removed and Rodrigo hung it in the corner of the storeroom, over the battered desk he referred to as his office.

The door to the bar scratched open and Cesar—a regular—came in, with a guilty look on his face. Not for what he'd done, but for what he was about to do. Cesar tended to approach life crab-like, in a series of side-to-side movements that eventually got him where he wanted to be. He was short, with a soft belly hiding his belt,

Cesar took a stool in front of Rodrigo and took off his straw fedora and laid it on the bar, revealing a head of black hair worn an inch too long for his small-featured face. He put both hands palm down on the bar.

Rodrigo stared at the backs of Cesar's hands. Even palms down on the bar they trembled.

"Again?" said Rodrigo

"I'll have money tomorrow," said Cesar. "Maybe even tonight."

"How long have I known you?"

Cesar thought for a moment. "I don't know."

Rodrigo took a dog-eared notebook from under the counter and flipped through the pages. "Here it is. February 27, 2008. The first time you came into the bar. Which was also the first time you asked for credit. I gave it to you and you paid me back."

"First impressions," said Cesar.

Rodrigo frowned. "There were other times you didn't pay."

Cesar said nothing in reply. He had a finely honed sense of when to remain silent.

"The fault is mine," said Rodrigo. "There was no collateral for those loans."

"Just one drink. You can even pour El Cabrito. I don't mind."

Another man came in, an elderly *campesino*— Manolo—with raw hands and an errant mustache. He looked at Rodrigo and Cesar and said, "*Chinga. He's at it again?*"

"Buy me a shot," said Cesar, to Manolo.

"I buy *putas* a drink, not you."

Rodrigo turned away to rinse glasses in the sink. *All these people, flowing through here each day. I feel like I'm at the bank of the river that runs past the dump, watching trash bob and roll as it passes by. But there's no empty space in a river.*

Rodrigo reached out one finger and touched Cesar's straw fedora where it sat on the bar.

"My hat," said Cesar, not liking Rodrigo's gesture.

"I'll pour you a double," said Rodrigo. "And take your hat as collateral. You come back and pay me for the drink, your hat will be returned."

Cesar touched his head, feeling naked.

"Okay," said Cesar.

When Cesar was gone, Rodrigo came out from behind the bar. He picked up the fedora and hung it on the masonry nail on the blank wall, where the calendar once hung.

"That's the last you'll see of that *cabron*," said Manolo.

Rodrigo took a step back. Looking at the hat, he felt he was seeing something important, but he didn't know what it was.

81

"He'll be back," said Rodrigo. "But not for the hat."

*

It was two a.m. when Rodrigo climbed the stairs to his apartment. He lived above the bar, on the second floor. He lit a single lamp and passed back and forth in the shadows. The quarters were small, but the lack of furniture made them look more spacious than they were. There was a tiny bedroom, a toilet, a space for eating and sitting, and a compressed kitchen area.

No one ever came to the apartment. Some men make friends easily but it wasn't one of Rodrigo's talents. When he needed sexual relief—which was infrequent at his age—56—he went to a bordello on Calle Once.

Was he lonely? It was indisputable he was alone.

Rodrigo took a plastic pitcher from the fridge and poured a glass of *tamarindo* juice. When the glass was empty, he bent over the kitchen sink and washed the smoke of other people's cigarettes from his face, and then settled into bed. The street was silent outside.

A hat. A hat on the wall. What else is needed?

*

It didn't take long for the news to make the rounds of his regulars—that Rodrigo gave credit if you provided collateral. But not just any collateral—it

82

would have to be an item of clothing, and it was Rodrigo who would make the choice.

Some famous drunks appeared with clothing they'd filched from a relative. It was of no concern to Rodrigo where the clothing came from, as long as they were pieces to complete the figure of a man he was building on the formerly empty wall. Cesar's straw fedora was joined by a pair of jockey briefs, a sweat-stained undershirt, a ripped chambray work shirt, green polyester pants, work gloves and work boots, and a cheap watch for an imaginary wrist.

When the figure was fully clothed, Rodrigo sat back and waited. If someone asked if he was finished, he'd say no. He needed a face.

*

Word spread around town. A city as big as Mexicali has plenty of hopeless men who have succumbed to drugs, alcohol, and failure. Rodrigo was fond of saying, "The criminal mind has no sense of consequence, and no sense of time."

*

They came in together late at night. Two drinkers. The other men at the bar stared as the two men found empty stools. No one had ever seen them before.

One of them was pale—paler than most Mexicans, with green eyes. Rodrigo wondered if he might be part German.

The other was an old *cholo* with prison tattoos—too old for the clothes he wore—the *cholo* uniform of long shorts and calf-covering white socks. The old *cholo's* eyes drooped pouches of loose skin. His hair was buzzed short and the stubble he'd missed was gray.

Rodrigo walked along the duckboards and stood in front of the two strangers. He waited but they remained silent and Rodrigo finally said, "Drink?"

"That depends," said the pale one.

"We heard a story," said the *cholo*. His voice was ragged and wheezy, as though he'd been hit in the throat.

"The bus station has seats where you can sit all night," said Rodrigo. "Here you have to drink."

The pale one said, "We want two bottles of tequila each. Jimador."

"This isn't a nightclub," said Rodrigo. "We don't sell bottles."

"If what they say is true," said the pale one, "you'll give us what we ask."

The pale one reached his hand up to his face and with a gentle tug removed a glass eye. He set it down on the bar where it looked wetly up at Rodrigo.

The *cholo* stuck his fingers in his mouth and pulled out a full set of dentures. In the space of a second, the *cholo* aged twenty years. He set the teeth down next to the eye.

"Do we have a deal?" asked the pale one.

*

Strangers began coming into the bar to see the man on the wall. Its head was perplexing since Cesar's straw fedora hat lay flat above a single glass eye and a stained set of teeth. One academic wandered in and judged the arrangement "cubist." Some newcomers came in for a look and quickly left. A few of the younger men, in skinny jeans and hoodies, took selfies with their phones.

The bar's regulars ignored the man on the wall and concentrated on the drinks in front of them.

Rodrigo dubbed his creation, El Borracho. The Drunk.

*

The pillow clung to Rodrigo's cheek, wet with sweat. He flipped it over with one hand and felt wetness there, too, and realized he'd reversed the pillow an hour earlier.

There was no air conditioning in Rodrigo's bedroom—only a rotating fan that made a clatter and clunk when it shifted on its base. Rodrigo lay flat on his back, unable to sleep, taking sips of water from a plastic jug by the side of his bed.

He got up, stepped into his flip-flops, and dressed in a thin bathrobe. At first, he thought he was getting up for no reason—maybe to stare out the window, hoping to convince himself to lie down again and this time slip deep into sleep. So, it came as a surprise when he opened the door and walked down the stairs to the interior door to El Chupacabra.

Instead of turning on the lights, he lit three *veladoras*, tall candles in glass he kept for those occasions when the city's electricity failed. The three *veladoras* were imprinted with images of Catholic saints: San Michael, San Raymond, and San Martin. The tall candles shed a trembling light, giving rudimentary animation to the man on the wall.

Rodrigo poured two tall shots of his best Jimador. He lifted one glass and clinked it against the other. He glanced at El Borracho and said, "Salud, mi amigo."

A sip and the sensation of tequila burning the back of his throat.

El Borracho spoke with a click of teeth, asking "Are you an educated man?"

Rodrigo considered the question, then replied, "It wasn't my fortune to be educated."

"What about me?" said El Borracho. "I have no fortune at all."

"No debts either," said Rodrigo. "And no failures."

"And you think that is a good thing? Living with a broken scale?"

"I give you a roof over your head," said Rodrigo. "That's more than was ever given me."

The candles guttered in a breeze from an open window and for a moment El Borracho's face was in shadow.

"How do you live?" asked El Borracho.

"What do you mean?"

"Your rooms upstairs. How do you live?"

Rodrigo thought for a moment.

"Quietly."

"You never go to the ocean?" asked El Borracho.

"There's no ocean here."

"Mountains?"

"La Rumorosa. Not so far away."

"But still, you spend every day here, and every night alone."

"Not every night."

There was the bordello. But that business was done in an hour. Then he was home again.

The collar of El Borracho's shirt fluttered in a breeze from the same window that disturbed the candles.

"You don't understand what I'm saying," said the man on the wall.

Rodrigo looked down at El Borracho's glass of tequila and saw the surface ripple in concentric rings.

*

It was three weeks after the man on the wall was complete, that the pale one returned to El Chupacabra. This time he came alone. He wore a smudged gauze bandage taped over one eye.

"I've come to settle my debt," the pale one said.

Rodrigo shifted his gaze away from the pale one's green eye.

Rodrigo said, "You have the money to pay for two bottles of Jimador?"

"You sold me 750s. How much is that worth?"

Rodrigo gave him the price he'd pay in the Soriana supermarket. "Four hundred and forty pesos."

The pale one frowned. "That much?"

Rodrigo nodded.

The pale one dug into his pocket and came up with a combination of coins and notes. 440 pesos.

"I have it," he said. "I want my eye back."

Rodrigo took a deep breath and let it out slowly. He reached to the top shelf and took down a bottle of Patrón. It was rare that he poured such expensive tequila. It was reserved for regulars celebrating special days—a birthday, a wedding, a christening.

He set the bottle down in front of the pale one. "You are the only one who ever came back to claim his collateral. Much respect."

The pale one pushed the coins and notes across the bar. "First, take my money."

"Of course."

Rodrigo gathered the cash and sorted it into the cash register. He then poured a double shot for the pale one. "Drink up, amigo. On the house."

It took three hours and for much of that time, Rodrigo thought he'd made a tactical error. But the pale one had the greed of the poor and made the most of his good fortune, downing one shot after another. When he was bleary-eyed and talking nonsense, when his gauze bandage slipped to reveal an empty and scarred socket, Rodrigo switched to a plastic bottle of De Caña Tonayan, a drink he rarely served, since there was no profit in it. It was a cheap, overproof liquor made of sugarcane and agave and swallowed by only the most desperate drunks.

The pale one didn't notice the switch. He didn't notice much at all.

When he stood, he collapsed on the floor.

No one could rouse him. When the ambulance finally came—more than an hour after being called—the white-suited attendants carried the pale one out the door.

Rodrigo wasn't surprised when the news got back to him the next day—that the pale one had died in the night. No autopsy or reason for the death.

Manolo had shrugged and said, "His life killed him."

*

When the doors were closed for the night and the bar wiped clean one last time, Rodrigo poured his now customary two shots of tequila. One for himself; one for the man on the wall.

Empty of people, the bar seemed even smaller. This didn't make sense to Rodrigo, but he had to acknowledge it was true.

"Salud," said Rodrigo, lifting his glass.

There was a long moment of silence between the two. The comfortable silence between two friends.

"I would have hated to have lost my eye," said El Borracho.

"That won't happen now."

"No one cried for him. The pale one."

"I've had this bar for twenty-seven years," said Rodrigo. "Some men can raise the bottle and set it down. Some men pour and never stop. You've seen Manolo. He comes in for one Tecate and a shot of Jimador. Never more than that. He stays an hour and goes home to his wife. I hear his sons and daughters and grandchildren visit him every Sunday. They do a carne asada in the backyard. A man could work hard if he had Sundays like those."

"Living alone is not a life," said El Borracho. *"It's a life of crumbs."*

"You're not alone," said Rodrigo.

The candlelight reflected in El Borracho's sole eye.

"We are both alone."

*

The woman came in an hour before closing. Rodrigo noticed she fumbled as she took her seat at the bar and placed her purse in front of her. There was a somnambulism to her movements and Rodrigo wondered if she was already drunk. All of the regulars took note of her but none spoke. It was unusual to see a woman at the bar. If she was a *puta* she was an odd one. Well into middle-age, maybe older. Black hair streaked with gray, with a rhinestone clip holding it to one side. Her eyes were brown with vivid whites and heavily made-up with shadow and mascara. Her lips were stark red, large and full—perhaps too full for her face. Her dress was extravagant and colorful, with splashes of tropical colors. The dress was tight enough that it hinted at mature curves under the fabric. Unusual for a warm night, she wore white cloth gloves.

Rodrigo didn't serve her immediately, in case she realized she'd stumbled into the wrong cantina for a woman alone.

The heat from the day had never left and even now, after midnight, there was a close warmth in the air, the kind that draws out beads of sweat on a forearm or upper lip.

The woman stared Rodrigo's way, a signal to be served.

He took a few steps to where she sat.

"Two Jimadors," she said.

"Two?"

For a moment, Rodrigo wondered if he had been observed conversing with El Borracho; if the woman's presence was a prank devised by the regulars.

The woman gave a shake to her head. "No. A double, not two."

Rodrigo poured and watched as she gulped the tequila down in one go.

She set the glass down with a knock and said, "Another."

When the second disappeared as quickly as the first, Rodrigo leaned forward and said in confidential tones, "Senora, are you all right?"

Instead of answering, she looked over her shoulder at the man on the wall and said, "What is his name?"

"I call him El Borracho."

She pointed at her empty glass. "Another."

*

The hour passed and one by one the regulars shuffled out the door. The woman stayed.

She said to Rodrigo, "I'm not done."

Rodrigo reached under the table and took out the three candles with the images of the saints. He lit them and then flicked off the lights. He didn't want any die-hard drunks banging on the door, seeing the light and thinking he was open.

"You're drinking too much," said Rodrigo. "I don't want to kill you."

The woman had spoken little over the course of the hour. Now, she said, "They already killed me." She seemed poised to launch into a tale of woe, then stopped herself.

"Bring me water," she said.

Rodrigo poured a tall glass from a ceramic pitcher and handed it to her.

The 200-peso note she had laid on the bar was depleted to a five-peso coin. That didn't stop Rodrigo from continuing to serve her one double after another.

"What is your name," he said.

"Isla."

Rodrigo attempted some humor, saying, "No man is an island."

Isla let out a soft puff of a laugh. "No woman either."

Rodrigo thought, *"What is cruelty?"*

He pointed at the five-peso coin. "You need to put more money on the bar."

Isla glanced at her purse. "I don't have any more."

Is this a gift? Or am I seizing what is mine?

Rodrigo looked at the woman's hands, her neck, the lobes of her ears. No jewelry. No collateral except her clothing.

"We have a custom here," he said. "of taking collateral for drinks."

"I know," she said.

"Clothing."

She nodded. "I wore a dress that would please El Borracho."

Rodrigo had seen it before, on a science show on TV. Timelapse photography of a beautiful flower growing before his eyes. The seed, the translucent stem, the first tender leaves, the bud and the bloom.

It was like that with Isla. With each drink, another item of clothing was shed. Rodrigo took his heavy hammer and masonry nails and piece-by-piece formed a woman next to El Borracho—a bride that could match El Borracho drink for drink.

When he had nailed the last piece of clothing he turned and regarded Isla sitting on the stool, naked. Each crease of flesh, each dimple and scar were a testament to her beauty.

"Finished," said Rodrigo.

"No," said Isla

Isla rummaged in her purse. She got up from the stool and stood in front of the woman on the wall. With blush, she smeared an oval in the empty space under the hair clip and above the neckline of the color-splashed dress. With mascara, she drew two eyes. With her lipstick an unsmiling mouth.

Both figures on the wall had outstretched hands, but the gloved fingers of the woman on the wall fell inches short of the work glove of El Borracho.

"She needs a name," said Rodrigo.

"Don't call her La Borracha," said Isla.

Rodrigo shook his head, "Her name is El Regalo."

The Gift.

*

They twisted together in bed. Both naked. The sheets underneath them soaked in sweat, in cum, in drippings from her vagina.

When he mounted her the second time, he closed his eyes and conjured he was El Borracho, with one green eye and clicking teeth. He pressed his face against her cheek, imagining he was pressing against an oval, with crudely drawn eyes and lips. When he climaxed, he felt a discharge from the base of his spine.

"Water," said Isla.

Rodrigo got up from bed and walked into the kitchen and filled a tall glass with water. He handed it to Isla, who gulped half of it down without stopping.

She handed him the glass and laid back on the bed, closing her eyes. "Tomorrow, will you bring me clothes?"

"Will you stay?"

"I'm nailed to the wall."

Rodrigo lay next to her. His hand reached out but stopped within inches of touching hers.

"Not me," he said, teeth clicking in his mouth.

AN ILLUSION TO ME NOW

Jeff Esterholm

Stan McGregor sat at his realty office desk on Saturday, waiting for a one o'clock appointment. The Abelsons, a couple from out of town, retirees, wanted to move back to the wife's hometown, or near it, and were making the four-plus hour trip up from the Madison area that morning. McGregor had met them before, a happy sort, easy to laugh, wanting a change, and believing the cost of living was lower here in the northwestern corner of the state. Perhaps it was, but McGregor knew that every change had its cost.

The coffee maker, rimed with dust, sat on the credenza, the dry pot's insides, unwashed and unrinsed, clouded from hard water and past off-brand brews. These days, McGregor used a pod-per-cup machine which he tended to get a touch of the guilts over. All those used pods in the landfill alongside the lake. McGregor didn't want to get going on that topic, why the city ever opened a dump by Lake Superior he could never fathom. The payback for the past is always in the future. He finished a daily word game on his phone and turned the device face down. McGregor reasoned, we pay in our dotage—he was, he thought, a youthful seventy—and if we don't pay, surely the next and future generations would.

That rare, beautiful June day, traffic streamed north and south beyond the office's picture window, the parking lot empty except for the Jeep he would do the northland circuit in with the Abelsons that afternoon. There was a log home in the woods near Pattison Park that had attracted them. On the market too long, McGregor thought, but the Abelsons were interested. At just over four hundred, he would not be disappointed if they put in an offer.

He was about to text his wife, checking in, when she might expect him, when the Ablesons pulled up in their Prius, followed seconds later by another couple. McGregor glanced at the calendar on his phone: No. He wasn't expecting anyone else. Only the Abelsons. But then he looked again at the younger couple in their midnight blue BMW, an older model, well taken care of.

McGregor strolled out the agency's door as the Abelsons climbed from their vehicle. They were all smiles—Jerry Abelson had that familiar look of urgency after a long drive and too much coffee and water, so the real estate agent returned the smiles and nodded him back into the office. "You know where it is, Jerry. We'll be taking my Jeep." He welcomed Sylvia with a good afternoon and handshake while his eyes remained on the late arrivals, and then he nodded at them. the young couple, as well. McGregor's nod wasn't furtive, and Sylvia, along with Jerry, air drying his hands, patting them on his jeans, went on as if to show that this was *their* time with Stan McGregor and no one else's.

Sylvia had a print out of the log cabin's listing and waved it at McGregor.

He laughed. "Yes, yes. It's all set up. We have plenty of time. The property is fifteen miles south of here."

The young couple looked at each other—an attuned roll of the eyes, a work-with-me forbearance—and got back in the BMW and waited. McGregor sighed, then ushered Jerry and Sylvia to the Jeep with the realty agency's signs on the driver and passenger doors.

McGregor pulled out onto Highway 35 with the Abelsons in tow, the BMW following a car-length behind. Jerry, Sylvia, neither mentioned the other couple. McGregor knew better now, but if he were a different age, younger, still had a wild hair, and without clients in his care, he would have lost the shadowing car, turned off on a winding road east of Greenwood Cemetery, and these lost adult children.

"Are they friends of yours?" he finally asked. He already knew the answer. He wanted to check what the Abelsons might have seen.

Jerry leaned forward from the backseat. "What?"

Sylvia lost her smile, looked away, looked straight ahead.

Jerry looked back. The road behind was empty, wide open.

McGregor shook his head. "I thought there was a car behind us. A couple from the office parking lot." He couldn't stop himself. "With a BMW. Pulled up by you when you arrived?"

"Strange," Sylvia said. "Our son has a BMW."

"Mine too. The last I heard anyway."

"He did. Anyway. Couldn't say now," Sylvia continued. "It's been a while."

Jerry said, "Three years and four months to be exact. Since we all talked."

McGregor glanced in the rearview mirror. Jerry Abelson's lips were a welded line. He was through talking about it. McGregor knew that feeling. That's the way it was. "I'm sorry," McGregor said, and he was. "I haven't heard from my son or his wife in six years." He didn't add that he no longer expected to hear anything from them.

McGregor knew his son wasn't dead. He had heard over the years from relatives Daniel and Caitlin continued speaking to that his son and daughter-in-law may have moved to the Twin Cities—Minneapolis or St. Paul, no one knew for sure, or didn't want to say. Neither was dead, yet with their estrangement, McGregor thought of them that way, so that he could live. His wife managed in her own way.

The couple was illusory to him now. Daniel and Caitlin were ghosts that he would occasionally put out of his mind, only to have them reappear, trailing behind, unwilling to be known, unwilling to be forgotten.

THE DUST BRED BOB DYLAN

Adam Van Winkle

Woody was a singer
Songster
Songbird
Chanteur
Chanter
Warbler
Yodeler
Artiste

Woody was a writer
Woody was a poet
Woody was the father of Bob

Woodrow Guthrie was the son of
John Steinbeck and the twenty-eighth president

And when he sat and quivered
Because of the ailment that killed him
Woody had a mask for the disease
Of drink that he had long before

He was a wreck from the wreckage of the Dust
Bowl
A real man that made himself in actuality a fiction
A story of mythic proportion bigger than Texas
And small enough for a single bed at Greystone

Mermaid Avenue
California
Fruit Cove
Beluthahatchee
Beach Haven at Gravesend

He lived in more places than he had wives
Barely

And while he was barely alive
Just before he died
He still tasted the dust
That shit was indeed blowin in the wind

AIN'T ME

Matthew J. Andrews

Having left the suffocation of the city, Bob Dylan sits around a campfire, surrounded by strangers. He holds his hands to the fire for warmth and watches the shapes made by his breath. "You're Bob Dylan," a woman says to him. "I don't even know who that is," Bob Dylan responds. "You look just like him," a man says. "I'm not," Bob Dylan pleads, "Please let me be." "You must be him," says a little girl, "Your voice gives you away." "I swear to you," Bob Dylan says, "I don't know the man." In the distance, a rooster crows, and everyone but Bob Dylan begins to sob.

OPOSSUM

Zach Murphy

Pete and Richard's orange safety vests glowed a blinding light under the scorching sun, and their sweat dripped onto the pavement as they stood in the middle of the right lane on Highway 61, staring at an opossum lying stiffly on its side.

Richard handed Pete a dirty shovel. "Scoop it up," he said.

Everything made Pete queasy. He once fainted at the sight of a moldy loaf of bread. Even so, he decided to take on a thankless summer job as a roadkill cleaner. At least he didn't have to deal with many people.

Richard nudged Pete. "What are you waiting for?" he asked.

Pete squinted at the creature. "It's not dead," he said. "It's just sleeping."

"Are you sure?" Richard asked as he scratched his beard. He had one of those beards that looked like it would give a chainsaw a difficult time.

"Yes," Pete said. "I just saw it twitch."

Richard walked back toward the shoulder of the road and popped open the driver's side door of a rusty pickup truck. "Alright, let's go."

Pete shook his head. "We can't just leave it here."

"It's not our problem," Richard said. "They tell us to do with the dead ones, but not the ones that are still alive."

Pete crouched down and took a closer look. "We need to get it to safety," he said.

Richard sighed and walked back toward the opossum. "What if it wakes up and attacks us?" he asked. "That thing could have rabies."

"I don't think anything could wake it up right now," Pete said.

Richard belched, "It's an ugly son of a gun, isn't it?"

"I think it's so ugly that it's cute," Pete said.

"No one ever says that about me," Richard said with a chuckle. "I guess I just haven't crossed into that territory."

Just then, a car sped by and swerved over into the next lane. Pete and Richard dashed out of the way.

"People drive like animals!" Richard said. "We'd better get going."

Pete took a deep breath, slipped his gloves on, gently picked up the opossum, and carried it into the woods.

"What are you doing?" Richard asked. "Are you crazy?"

After nestling the possum into a bush, Pete smelled the scent of burning wood. He gazed out into the clearing and noticed a plume of black smoke billowing into the sky. The sparrows scattered away, and the trees stood with their limbs spread, as if they were about to be crucified.

"Jesus Christ," Pete whispered under his breath.

Pete picked up the opossum and turned back around.

SKETCH OF BOB DYLAN

Viola LaBounty

JUST LIKE A WOMAN

A. A. Rubin

As I wait for her to get ready, I stand out, inside the rain, staring at the empty porch.

Her life flashes in front of my eyes, snapshots of the past, like the thousands of photographs her mother insisted on taking—to remember (as if I'd ever forget)—in front of that red, weather-beaten front door. I remember the moment I placed her car seat down to open the door after she came home from the hospital, and she looked up at me for the first time with those big, little girl eyes. I knew that from that moment forward, I would brave anything for her and never feel any pain; the first day of school, all done up in her ribbons and her bows, the big backpack and the bigger dress; the first day of little league; dance recitals and gymnastics competitions, science fairs, graduation, and prom.

I remember sighing each time, proud of her as grew up, but hoping against logic and reality that she would stay forever young.

I remember the quiet times too, moments framed only in memory, when we sat together on that now-empty swing staring at the constellations, when I posed for her as she painted her water-color masterpieces, how we talked about everything and

110

anything in our own special place just outside the house, but miles away from her mother, brothers, and everyone else in the world.

I remember how I held her when she needed comfort, the surprising strength in her vise-like embraces, the beat of her heart against mine, the heat of her tears on my shoulder, and the questions in those big, little girl eyes as she looked into mine asking if it was going to be ok. I remember trying to assure her, trying to seem strong and certain. I remember wondering if she could feel my doubt.

I see her shadow behind the diaphanous drapes, moving toward the front door. My breath catches, as I see the knob turn, and wait for her to step out.

And when I see her standing there in that white dress looking just like a woman, I break just like a little girl.

FOX THEATER

Dia VanGunten

In my mind, a zaftig moon is a shining spoon and we're in a permissive mood, but poetry tinkers with memory. Okay, a crescent, a thin sliver of light in a Detroit alleyway. A parked bus hummed and steamed. In the plume of 7 foxtails, we were hoping to get lucky.

The kitsunian name of the place—theater of the mythic trickster—is crucial.

We peered at a doorway: rectangle outlined in red. Two roadies took a cigarette break. A lighter flamed. We pressed our bodies to the chain link fence. *Psst. Can you let us in? We're old friends.* We repeated ourselves, dragging out the word "old," an L for every year. They raised dubious eyebrows and double checked before they met us at the gate.

We didn't look like groupies—Mom, two teens and a 10 year old—yet we were ushered through that glowing door. I brought a friend but I don't remember her outfit. I wore denim cut-offs and tights, black & white stripes like a Seuss character. Red lipstick, a boy scouts beret and mary janes. Flats. (I'd winced through endless limping loops so that I could ditch my crutches.)

Mr. Tambourine Man jingle jangled. The awed crowd applauded. Zoe yawned. *Play a song for me. I'm not sleepy and there is no place I'm going to.* Rock stars don't impress my sister. A rolling trunk looked like a trundle. She clamored up and conked out. Someone laid their winter coat like a blanket. She slept through two encores but she was awake when Dylan left the stage. She saw me lift my head as he veered towards me. They steered him out the door, towards a waiting bus. He craned his neck to look back, a turning wheel.

The headliner was more comfortable in his bus so he slept in Hilton's parking lot. Mom got his unused hotel room. She smoked a joint with old friends while we swanned through the lobby, backstage passes plastered to our chests. We met teenage girls with passes of their own -- New Kids On The Block. They'd followed the boy band across the country. There was a series of hotel phone numbers. Sometimes the kids would answer and sometimes they wouldn't.

In Amish country, at a roadside diner, Dad sold us on dessert: fat slices of blueberry pie. Zoe passed Thom a shiny spoon and I sang a few lines. Dad let it slip then.

"Remember when Bob Dylan wanted to meet up with you? He wanted my permission. I told him he'd have an easier time getting a cold stick of butter up a wild cat's ass.

Thom sang in sandpaper twang: "I just want a chaaaaance to get into Dia's paaaaants."

Zoe and I exchanged looks. We were wary hippy kids. We knew a weird vibe when we felt it. I'd stored the memory in a logical spot. It belongs with the other animal encounters: fox at the crossroads, blinking owl in a high branch. A besotted toddler. A merciful rattlesnake. I keep Bob Dylan nestled next to a sullen silverback. A tenderness passed between us—gorilla and girl, both stuck. The silverback rose and approached. I knew the plan before it happened. When he pressed his lips to the glass, I leaned in for a kiss.

BOB DYLAN PIECE

David Lambert

CONTRIBUTORS

Matthew Ingate lives in London, plays the piano and guitar and works in the music industry. He is the author of *Together Through Life: My Never Ending Tour With Bob Dylan*, which chronicles over ten years on the road with Bob Dylan from 2011-2022.

Reagan M. Sova is an American writer living in Belgium. Described by one blogger as "a sharp-shooting Lone Ranger of the literary underground," Sova is the author of the critically acclaimed *Wildcat Dreams in the Death Light*, an 80,000-word mostly unpunctuated epic poem, published in 2022 by First to Knock.

Clem Flowers (They/ Them) is a poet, soft-spoken southern transplant, low rent aesthete, pizza man lover, gorgeous monstrosity, satanic mechanic & dramatic tenor living in Home of Truth, Utah with their awesome wife & sweet kitty. Hella queer & Non-binary poetry editor at *Blue River Review*, Pushcart & Best of the Net nominee, with publication credits including: *Olney Magazine*, *The Madrigal*, *Pink Plastic House Journal*, *Bullshit Lit*, *Corporeal*, *Holyflea*, *Anti-Heroin Chic*, *Messy Misfitsclub* & *Warning Lines Magazine*. Author of chapbooks *Stoked & Thrashing* (Alien Buddha Press,) *eating rain//matchstick graveyard* (Alien Buddha Press,) *Two Out of Three Falls* (Bullshit Lit,) *Snakeskin Stockings* (kith books,) & *Motel Neon* (back room poetry). Found on Twitter @clem_flowers

Michael Chin was born and raised in Utica, New York and currently lives in Las Vegas with his wife and son. His debut novel, *My Grandfather's an Immigrant and So is Yours* (Cowboy Jamboree Press) came out in 2021, and he is the author of three previous full-length short story collections. His essay collection, *Stories Wrestling Can Tell*, is forthcoming in 2023. Find him online at miketchin.com and follow him on Twitter @miketchin.

Daren Dean is the author of three novels and a short story collection. His fifth book, *ROADS*, is a novel forthcoming in February 2023 from CJ Press. Dean earned an MFA from the University of North Carolina at Wilmington. His short fiction has been nominated for the Pushcart Prize three times. *The Black Harvest: A Novel of The American Civil War* (University of West Alabama's Livingston Press, 2021) was nominated for the Pen/Faulkner, the W. Y. Boyd Literary Award for Excellence in Military Fiction, Midlands Author Award, and shortlisted for the Missouri Author Award. He is currently an Assistant Professor in English and Creative Writing at Lincoln University of Missouri where he was recently awarded the "Excellence in Scholarship Award" from the College of Arts and Sciences.

Patricia Q. Bidar is a working-class writer from San Pedro, California, with family roots in New Mexico, Arizona, and Utah. She is an alum of the U.C. Davis Graduate Writing Program and also holds a BA in

Filmmaking. Patricia's stories have appeared in *SmokeLong Quarterly, Wigleaf, Sou'wester, Little Patuxent Review,* and *Pidgeonholes,* among other places. Patricia's work has been nominated three times for the Pushcart Prize and has also garnered nominations for Best of the Net, Best Small Fictions, and Best Microfiction. When she is not writing fiction, Patricia reads, enjoys nature, and ghostwrites for nonprofit organizations. She lives with her family outside of Oakland, CA.

John Waddy Bullion's writing has appeared in *BULL, HAD, Maudlin House, Rejection Letters,* and *Identity Theory,* among other fine places. He lives in Fort Worth, Texas, with his family.

New York interdisciplinary artist **Amy Bassin** and writer **Mark Blickley** work together on text-based art collaborations and experimental videos. Their work has appeared in many national and international publications as well as two books, *Weathered Reports: Trump Surrogate Quotes from the Underground'* (Moria Books, Chicago) and *Dream Streams* (Clare Songbird Publishing House, New York). Their videos, *Speaking In Bootongue* and *Widow's Peek: The Kiss of Death* represented the United States in the 2020 year-long world tour of *Time Is Love: Universal Feelings: Myths & Conjunctions,* organized by the esteemed Togolese-French curator, Kisito Assangni. In 2022, Bassin exhibited work at New York's annual *Spring Break Art Fair* in an exhibition titled and based on

Blickley's text, "Real Realism: An Art Manifesto for the Disenchanted," curated by Laura Horne. https://www.amybassin.com/.

Mark Rogers is a writer and artist whose literary heroes include Charles Bukowski, Willy Vlautin, and Charles Portis. He lives in Baja California, Mexico with his Sinaloa-born wife, Sofia. His award-winning travel journalism for *USA Today* and other media outlets has brought him to 56 countries. His crime novels have been published in the U.S and UK. *Uppercut*, his memoir of moving to Mexico, is published by Cowboy Jamboree Press. NeoText publishes his *Tijuana Novels* series and *Gray Hunter* series.

Jeff Esterholm's work has previously appeared in Akashic Books's *Mondays Are Murder*, *Beat to a Pulp*, *Close to the Bone*, *Crime Factory*, *Mystery Tribune*, *Pulp Modern Flash*, *Rock and a Hard Place Magazine*, *Shotgun Honey*, *Tough*, and *Yellow Mama*. He received the Larry and Eleanor Sternig Award for Short Fiction from the Council for Wisconsin Writers in 2013. His short story collection will be published by Cornerstone Press, University of Wisconsin-Stevens Point, in November 2023.

Adam Van Winkle was born and raised in Texoma and currently resides with his wife and two sons in South Carolina. In addition to publishing his short fiction, poetry and creative nonfiction online and in print at places like *Pithead Chapel*, *Cheap Pop!*, *BULL*

Magazine, The Dead Mule School of Southern Literature, The Gorko Gazette, Roi Faineant Press and *Red Dirt Forum,* he has published several novels and plays with Red Dirt Press, Cowboy Jamboree Press, and Leftover Books. Van Winkle is named for the oldest Cartwright son on *Bonanza.* Find him and his publications online at www.adamvanwinkle.com and @gritvanwinkle.

Matthew J. Andrews is a private investigator and writer. He is the author of *I Close My Eyes and I Almost Remember,* and his work has appeared in *Rust + Moth, Pithead Chapel,* and *EcoTheo Review,* among others. He can be contacted at matthewjandrews.com.

Zach Murphy is a Hawaii-born writer with a background in cinema. His stories appear in *Reed Magazine, Still Point Arts Quarterly, The Coachella Review, Maudlin House, B O D Y, Litro Magazine,* and *Flash: The International Short-Short Story Magazine.* His chapbooks *Tiny Universes* (Selcouth Station Press, 2021) and *If We Keep Moving* (Ghost City Press, 2022) are available in paperback and ebook. He lives with his wonderful wife, Kelly, in St. Paul, Minnesota.

Viola LaBounty is an active member of St Croix Writers Group, Lake Superior Writers, in the Northland & Write On the Edge & Poetry Journey, both in The Foothills in Yuma AZ. She's an artist & plays an acoustic-electric Autoharp & is in the process of learning some of Dylan's Gospel music as it touches her heart personally.

You may have heard **A. A. Rubin**'s name blowing in the wind, as he moves from town to town, like a rolling stone. He writes everything from formal poetry, to comics, literary fiction to science fiction and fantasy, and almost everything in between. His work has appeared recently in *Ahoy! Comics, Love Letters to Poe*, and *Flying Ketchup Press*. Right now, he can't read too good, don't send him no more letters, no (contact him, instead, as @TheSurrealAri on social media, or through his website, www.aarubin.com), unless, of course, you send them from Desolation Row.

Dia VanGunten focuses on intimate, character-centered storytelling. Sometimes that character is herself. Her current fiction project is a series of graphic novels. *Pink Zombie Rose* can be read at *Apple In The Dark, Caustic Frolic, Fatal Flaw, Funemployment Press, Open Sewers, NoNothing Magazine, 100 Subtexts*, and *Viridian Door's X*. Many of these stories are illustrated by comic artist Beppi. VanGunten is on staff at outlander for memoir. Her CNF can also be found in *Caustic Frolic, Cream Scene Carnival, Cringe, Deadbeat Poets, Dreams In Hiding, In The Mood Magazine, Kinda Weird Mag, Polyester, Run Amok Books, Soft Star* and *Solstice Lit*. She is co-editor of online culture mag, *Cream Scene Carnival*. For more, see Instagram @pinkzombierose or www.pinkzombierose.com.

Cowboy Jamboree Press

Find **David Lambert** @davidlambertart on Twitter/Facebook/Patreon/Instagram.

Bob Dylan continues touring to this day at the age of 81.

Made in the USA
Columbia, SC
29 December 2022